Advance Praise for Primal Screams

"A well-researched, powerfully argued, and profound account of the deepest sources of our current cultural crises. Wise and courageous, Mary Eberstadt has written an indispensable book for understanding our time."

—**Leon R. Kass**, professor emeritus,
Committee on Social Thought, The University of Chicago

"*Primal Scream*s is a deeply thought-provoking reflection on human nature and the fate of our republic."

—**Mary Ann Glendon**, Learned Hand Professor
of Law, Harvard University

"Some basic questions of identity have overtaken Western politics in the twenty-first century, and before they can be addressed, they must be understood. With her characteristic clarity and breadth of learning, Mary Eberstadt offers a powerfully persuasive guide to why we are beset by these challenges, and how to take them on."

—**Yuval Levin**, editor of *National Affairs*

"Mary Eberstadt proves, yet again, that she is one of America's most insightful—as well as compassionate—social analysts."

—**George Weigel**, Distinguished Senior Fellow and
William E. Simon Chair in Catholic Studies,
Ethics and Public Policy Center

"Mary Eberstadt understands 'identity politics' better than its practitioners—and any of its critics to date. She takes seriously the question of why so many people feel a need for the sense of belonging that identity politics seeks to provide. Her answer is terrifying—a loss that human beings of modern times have suffered, but of which we have been almost entirely unaware. Until now."

—**Tod Lindberg**, author of
The Heroic Heart: Greatness Ancient and Modern

"It is scarcely a foregone conclusion that our society will return to sanity on questions of sexual morality and marriage. But if we do, then prophets like Mary Eberstadt will be celebrated in song and story."

—**Robert P. George**, McCormick Professor of
Jurisprudence, Princeton University

"In *Primal Screams*, Mary Eberstadt responds to the deepest cries of the wounded souls of our time. Read it and share it."

—**Kathryn Jean Lopez**, National Review Institute

PRIMAL SCREAMS

PRIMAL SCREAMS

HOW THE SEXUAL REVOLUTION
CREATED IDENTITY POLITICS

Mary Eberstadt

TEMPLETON PRESS

Templeton Press
300 Conshohocken State Road, Suite 500
West Conshohocken, PA 19428
www.templetonpress.org

Set in Janson Text by Pro Production Graphic Services

Library of Congress Control Number: 2019943501

ISBN: 978-1-59947-411-3 (cloth: alk. paper)

This paper meets the requirements of ANSI/NISO Z39.48-1992
(Permanence of Paper).

A catalogue record for this book is available from the Library of Congress.

19 20 21 22 23   10 9 8 7 6 5 4 3 2 1

Printed in the United States of America.

For Nick

"If a man has lost a leg or an eye, he knows he has lost a leg or an eye; but if he has lost a self—himself—he cannot know it, because he is no longer there to know it."

—Oliver Sacks, *The Man Who Mistook His Wife for a Hat and Other Clinical Tales*

Contents

ix

Introduction

THE MYTH OF THE LONE WOLF

Once upon a time, a great many people held two common beliefs that science has now overruled.

One was that *Canis lupus*, Latin for wolf, commonly exists in isolation from other wolves—an assumption whose pedigree extends back centuries.[1] Another was that wolves roamed in "packs," meaning more or less random assortments of their species. Today, thanks in part to a thirteen-year study of the wolves on Ellesmere Island in the Northwest Territories by wildlife biologist L. David Mech, we now know that neither of these suppositions is true.[2]

Wolves are, in fact, intensely familial animals. Temple Grandin, an autistic savant and a professor and preeminent authority on animal behavior, summarizes the scientific turnaround with co-author Catherine Johnson as follows:

> Mech's findings turn practically everything we think we know about wolves upside down. . . . Wolves live the way

people do, in families made up of a mom, a dad, and their children. Sometimes an unrelated wolf can be adopted into a pack, or one of the mom's or dad's relatives is part of the pack (the "maiden aunt").... But mostly wolf packs are just a mom, a dad, and their pups.[3]

Such work documenting the mom-and-pop foundations of lupine life is one example of the ways in which new technologies and research are revealing just how social—in particular, how *familial*—animal life is. Ozzie and Harriet, a monogamous pair with offspring attached, is not always the norm. Surprisingly often, though, whether they mate for life or not, animals are now known to exist in kinship structures similar to those governing human beings from time immemorial, replete with mothers and fathers, siblings, extended family, and sometimes other female relatives, childless or otherwise, who help to raise the young.

New investigations into the social lives of animals also reveal this corollary: though many human beings might play today by the rules of the TV comedy *Modern Family*, according to which a "family" is whatever its self-appointed members say it is, other animals do not. Thus, by way of a few examples, what goes for wolves goes also for coyotes and many other mammals: they live in nuclear or extended biological families.[4] Orca offspring live with their parents all their lives.[5] Barring capture, female elephants stay with their mothers until one or the other dies, and baby elephants remain within some fifteen feet of their mothers for the first eight years of life.[6] Bottlenose dolphins can recognize related dolphins after being separated for twenty years.[7] And so on.

Of course there are deep reasons why animals have evolved to behave in such familial ways. In the matter of their need to "know" their own relatives from others, elemental forces are in play. One is the exigency to avoid inbreeding, which is inimical to long-term survival of the species, and against which animal life has accordingly devised strategies.[8] Another is that there is strength in numbers and cooperation for both predator and prey. In sum:

> Most complex animal societies are actually families in which group members are related and therefore share a high proportion of their genes. The cooperative and often complex collective action that arises from such family groups is a product of the interaction of individuals seeking to maximize their own evolutionary fitness.[9]

Other recent groundbreaking research has revealed that animals are *social learners* on a scale hitherto unknown.[10] Many of their cardinal lessons in life, those crucial to survival, are learned by observing and interacting with others of their kind—especially mothers and siblings. During the past decade, several species have been newly detected "teaching" their young, among them rock ants, meerkats, and southern pied babblers.[11] At the outermost edge of such learning, some birds even appear to learn their song in utero.[12]

Not surprisingly, our improved understanding of the social sophistication of fellow creatures is reverberating beyond animal science. New insight into the extraordinary characteristics of elephants is one reason why they're no longer found in circuses.[13] California has banned orca shows and breeding, SeaWorld is phasing them out, and other governing bodies are debating similar measures aimed at protecting these socially complex mammals.[14] Mexico City has outlawed dolphin performances and dolphinariums, and other sites engaging in such animal displays might follow suit.[15] Whatever else it brings, tomorrow seems destined to include more solicitude for animals than we've often seen in the past, thanks in large part to advancing empirical under-standings of their complicated communal lives.

Why did anyone believe in the myth of the "lone wolf" in the first place? Temple Grandin and Catherine Johnson theorize that people missed the truth initially because most research on wolves was done on animals in captivity. Animals in captivity—typically separated from their families and surrounded by nonrelated ani-mals in an unnatural setting—exhibit behaviors markedly dissimi-lar from those left in nature. These effects range from heightened anxieties and aggression to the development of "stereotypies," or compulsive repetitive tics, and other self-destructive habits that do not arise in the animal's native ecosystem.[16] Animals can indeed live in "forced packs" (i.e., among unrelated members of their kind). But it is in forced packs that problems of dominance and hierarchies become accentuated, as animals deprived of familial order must then develop new strategies for competition. Wolves living in families, explain Grandin and Johnson, do not have dominance fights.[17]

Of course the invocation of research into animal behavior for a book about identity and human beings is intrinsically limited. Thus, nothing in the pages ahead depends on the latest empirical leaps into understanding our fellow life-forms, though examples irresistible for purposes of illustration will appear here and there. All the same, and at no risk of "anthropomorphizing the animals" or "zoo-morphizing" the people, we might meditate for starters on the irony that science now puts before us.

The more human beings learn about the fantastically intri-cate social workings of nonhuman beings, the more some want to spare those fellow creatures suffering. This includes the pain of familial and habitat separation, and the dysfunctions associated with that dislocation: anxiety, repetitive behaviors, shorter life spans, self-harm.[18] At the same time, we live in an age when young people inside and outside the United States show a marked rise in anxiety and repetitive behaviors;[19] when American life expectancy has fallen four years in a row for the first time in recorded history in what has been called "a stunning reversal for a developed nation";[20] and when self-harm among the young is also on the rise—dramatically so.[21]

Does the surging human understanding of other species extend to our own?

This book is about some of the consequences—in particular, the political consequences—that have been visited on *Homo sapiens* since we made ourselves exceptions to rules that are part and parcel of the survival strategy of fellow creatures.

There are two propositions that the divided precincts of America can agree on—and these may be the only two such propositions. They are that the polity is divided, at times viciously, as never before in peacetime, and that identity politics is among the most potent political forces of our time.

Since the election of Donald Trump in 2016, so many books and articles have been written about both these transformations that hand-wringing has become a national cottage industry. From pundits and politicians to everyday bystanders, many inside and outside the United States intuit that the country has had a great fall. The arguments about its cause(s) are ever more rancorous. And no one seems to know how to fix what's broken, in large part because "what's broken" is itself a subject of acrimonious dispute.

Premonitions of social and political catastrophe abound. "In America, Talk Turns to Something Not Spoken of for 150 Years: Civil War," warned a 2019 headline in the *Washington Post*.[22]

Citing a "hyper-partisan atmosphere" and "a crumbling of confidence in the country's democratic institutions and its paralyzed federal government," the piece went on to quote forbidding forecasts of serious unrest by leading politicians and pundits. Similar grim assessments ricochet throughout the media. The *Atlantic* has foretold "the end of the American order."[23] *New York* magazine has described the United States as "ripe for tyranny."[24] *Project Syndicate* speaks of "Apocalypse Trump"[25] and is not alone.

This book takes note of the omnipresent foreboding of our time, and of the increasingly furious fights over politics, particularly identity politics. Rather than join those existing conversations, though, I wish to start a different one in the hope of engaging people across the political and cultural spectrums. It begins with a simple question: How has the matter of "identity" come to be emotional and political ground zero for so many in the first place?

First, a summary of the current scene.

As everyone knows, sexual identity, racial identity, ethnic identity, and the rest of the pack have become essential to leftist politics—so much so that imagining today's progressivism without these group identities or their agendas is an exercise in futility. The outcome of the next presidential election will be shaped like all other races on variables seen and unseen as of now; the renascence of socialism, for one, looms especially large. But it will also depend in large part on the struggle—already titanic within the liberal-left—between those who believe they can ride identity politics into victory, and those who demur.

Meanwhile, outside of national politics, ideologies of identity continue their spread into one cultural institution after another. Campuses across the Western world have become proscenia for the enactment of identity panic, complete with "safe spaces," "trigger warnings," "appropriation" conflicts, and other intriguing linguistic innovations that will be analyzed ahead. The shouting down of speakers with unwanted views has become routine, shakedowns in the form of demands for extra "security" funding for supposedly controversial guests are so common as to be unremarkable, and speech on the quad and elsewhere is policed down to the pronoun for transgressions offensive to one or another inflamed subset.

As the campuses go, so do other flagships, from vaunted cultural spaces like museums[26] to essential academic fields including science, technology, engineering, and math.[27] The human resources departments of corporations now operate in part as weaponized hall monitors, patrolling their bureaucracies and employees' social media accounts for transgressions against identitarian codes.[28] Fashion runways, Halloween, public bathrooms, libraries: it's hard to think of a quotidian venue that *hasn't* run afoul lately of prefix Puritans or "appropriation" scouts.

To acknowledge the ubiquity of identity politics today is not to suggest moral equivalence—or *immoral* equivalence—among any particular groups. Neither is it to suggest a monocausal theory of what unites them; as we shall see, the social forces in play are legion. But *pace* suggestions that identity politics is business as usual, it represents a tectonic shift. For many Americans and other citizens, political desires and political agendas have become indistinguishable from the desires and agendas of the particular aggrieved faction with which they most "identify"—and the human beings outside those chosen factions are treated more and more not as fellow citizens, but as enemies to be eliminated by shame, intimidation, and, where possible, legal punishment. That is something new.

Another fact familiar by now is that many other people deplore this unexpected and often incendiary new world.

The conservative-right side of the political spectrum, as

opposed to the minuscule alt-right, is nearly unanimous in opposing identity politics—at least as a matter of theory, if not always in practice. "Identity politics," says Fox News host Tucker Carlson by way of example, "will destroy this country faster than any foreign invasion."[29] University of Toronto psychologist Jordan B. Peterson calls identity politics "reprehensible."[30] Rod Dreher, author of *The Benedict Option*, describes it vividly as "the kind of thing that convinces a black female Yale student from a privileged background that she is a victim because of the color of her skin, and that some toothless white Appalachian man on disability is an oppressor, because of his."[31] According to the conservative critique, the unrelenting focus on identity infantilizes the polity, substitutes victimhood for citizenship, and subverts responsible self-government by turning *E pluribus unum* on its head, making many out of one.

What has also emerged during the past few years is that more than a few liberals agree with that analysis. Ethologist and evolutionary biologist Richard Dawkins has called identity politics "one of the great evils of our age."[32] Columbia University professor Mark Lilla, author of the anti-identitarian manifesto *The Once and Future Liberal*, argues that the ideology "fetishizes our individual and group attachments, applauds self-absorption, and casts a shadow of suspicion over any invocation of a universal democratic *we*."[33] Psychologist and professor Steven Pinker, another liberal critic, says that when identity politics "spreads beyond the target of combatting discrimination and oppression, it is an enemy of reason and Enlightenment values."[34]

In sum, the parties to the debate, pro and con, are evident enough. What has not yet been illuminated, however, is the wider story of which they are all part. Whichever way one looks—to the left or to the right, to culture or to politics, across the United States or across the pond—a remarkable fact appears: the question *Who am I?* is now one of the most fraught of our time. It has the natural habitat of the human animal, with radical results that we are only beginning to understand. Its argument is not about individual choices, but about the collective environmental impact of many millions of them, taken over the course of many years.

Decades into the unintended and potent experiment of the sexual revolution, a great many human beings now live as if we are not the intensely communal creatures that we always have been; and systemic consequences of that profound shift are now emerging. These include our increasingly surreal politics. To study the timeline is to see that identity politics has grown in tandem with the spread of the sexual revolution—and not only in the United States, but across every society rooted in Western civilization. In postrevolutionary societies, the old ways of knowing *who I am* and *what I'm for* (i.e., by reference to family, extended family, and real-life larger communities) are growing weaker for many people and no longer exist at all for some. For different reasons of modernity and postmodernity, all of these collective identities have deteriorated. In his landmark 2000 book *Bowling Alone*, political scientist Robert D. Putnam mapped the dislocations of declining communities and associations.[35] The analysis that follows examines the decline of the first among equals of these: the primary community of the family.

Outside of wartime or other catastrophe, the organic connections of this unit have been sundered as never before. Vague talk of "family change," of the kind that has become commonplace, does not do justice to the enormity of this reality. Empirical evidence, such as that presented in chapter 2, makes a start. Systemwide familial dislocations are now having repercussions at every stage of human life, as shown by new data about the steep rise in psychiatric problems among American teenagers and young adults; decades of empirical evidence about the harms of fatherless homes (a literature as well-known as it is stoutly ignored); the "loneliness studies" now proliferating in sociology, spotlighting the increasing isolation of the elderly in every Western nation; and troubling new evidence of the human costs of new techniques for making babies, such as anonymous sperm donation.

Chapter 3 moves on to other evidence suggesting the familial origins of today's existential panic, including the infantilized vernacular of identity politics itself. Chapters 4 and 5 show that postrevolutionary havoc has given rise to new social survival strategies, as people unmoored from kinship identity seek substitutes that will do what organic families exist to do (i.e., protect the individuals included in them).

If Western men and women are indeed more atomized and estranged from their own than ever before, then we would also expect to see evidence of a serious breakdown in one of the family's primary functions: social learning. Chapter 6 argues that the #MeToo movement still reverberating across the Western world is a case in point. Nonmarital sex is now less consequential and less stigmatized than ever before. But the shrinkage and implosion of the family has meanwhile crushed the petri dish through which previous generations learned about the opposite sex. The ironic result is that the most sexually *practiced* generation of humanity may also be the most sexually *illiterate*—a paradox that the example of #MeToo, with its incoherent Rashomon stories, bears out.

In short, the argument of this book is that today's clamor over identity—the authentic scream by so many for answers to questions about where they belong in the world—did not spring from nowhere. It is a squalling creature unique to our time, born of familial liquidation.[36]

To zero in on under-examined parts of the record is not to say that the effects of the revolution are distributed equally, or that they are equally injurious for all. Evolutionary winners have emerged alongside the ranks of the damaged, as will be considered in the book's conclusion. Neither is it to suggest that future renorming is impossible. To the contrary, there may be nascent signs of social turnaround here and there already, as we'll also see.

But if the United States, and the societies to which it is most closely related, are in as parlous shape as many people now believe, there will be no way out unless we call things by their correct names. The rote left/right memes of the times concerning "tribes" and "resistance," "intersectionality" and "elites" may be useful shorthand for punditry. But they do not strike to the root of what ails us. Informed analysis of the sexual revolution and its deleterious consequences does.

Some readers will object to putting our radically individualized familial order on center stage. Their reluctance is common. In fact, one reason why the sexual revolution is among the most challenging intellectual puzzles of our time is precisely because of the psychological resistance that its mere mention tends to generate—including and even especially among people who otherwise regard themselves as open-minded. This book appeals to all readers to put reflexive dismissal aside, and focus on the evidence. For purposes of this argument, it does not matter whether you lean left or right, progressive or conservative, apolitical or activist. What matters is only the desire to understand the massively altered habitat of our species, and how that transformation is reshaping Western society and politics.

The sexual revolution and its fallout are fair analytical game, because individual decisions multiplied by many millions continue to have massive public consequences. To name just two far-reaching examples beyond the purview of this book, these include the expansion of the Western welfare state, as it has been forced to become the substitute parent in broken homes; and the crisis of immigration in Europe, as governments in countries with fewer and fewer young workers due to demographic collapse have come to justify the importing of millions more as an economic necessity. Both trends are among the most momentous in the contemporary Western world, and neither can be understood apart from the role played by the sexual revolution in each.

Other readers may have a different reflexive reaction to the argument that is also familiar: fearing that what's afoot is a stealth attempt to "turn back the clock," "go back to the fifties," "put the genie back in the bottle," or otherwise engage in reactionary skullduggery. I would note, first, that the sheer number of clichés we have developed to describe such an action tells us something—namely, that a great many postrevolutionary people resist even a whiff of revisionism about laissez-faire sex. Second, to the extent that this book's argument might accurately be called "revisionist," it is also theoretical. This is an argument about ideas, not policies. Activists can make of it what they will. What is paramount, first, is the diagnosis.

To say that post-1960s levels of fatherlessness, divorce, shrinking families, and abortion, among other trends, have become major impediments to the understanding of self is not to say these are the *only* phenomena propelling identity politics. This brings us to a critical moral stipulation: that real crimes and injustices have been committed against real sexual and racial and other minorities—wrongs that have naturally driven many people to group identities in the hopes of preventing more wounds. Nothing in the argument of this book diminishes or sugarcoats that fact, or the sufferings behind it.

To illustrate by way of prominent example, the August 11, 2017, "Unite the Right" rally in Charlottesville, Virginia—in which one woman was killed and dozens of others were injured in the ensuing riot—shocked the country with the knowledge that some fraction of Americans, however small in number compared to everyone else, has embraced white nationalism. This tragedy joined other frightening examples of racism inside and outside the country's borders.[37] There is no doubt that America's original sin still coils and strikes, and not only in America. There never has been.

To say that the phenomenon of identity politics has more than one cause is not to minimize the importance of others. And just as family meltdown is not the only reason for identitarianism, so are there multiple causes behind other phenomena that play major roles in our national division quite aside from identity politics.

Consider the growth of populism within red states, whose causes identity-firsters seem not to understand. In parts of the country like the Rust Belt, apprehension abounds that illegal immigration might further reduce scarce working-class jobs. There and elsewhere, the opioid epidemic has carried off many loved ones and economic insecurity and other forms of hardship are rife—but many in blue America seem not to notice, except to denigrate the wounded, as President Barack Obama did, for "clinging" to guns and religion.[38] And quite apart from such class division, there is also legitimate fear in other precincts that rising antireligious prejudice is stifling freedom of religion and speech for those whom coastal progressives deem retrograde.[39] To write off as bigots and "deplorables" these millions of fellow citizens with authentic concerns of their own has added gratuitous insult to what is already, for many, the social injury of globalization.

As Douglas Murray has pointed out in *The Strange Death of Europe*, his sweeping analysis of the unprecedented recent immigration into countries across the Continent, many people there, mainly from the lower classes, resisted such extensive social change with little to no empathy from their leaders in government.[40] Arguments over immigration are not the same in Europe and the United States. But while both do share a link to the sexual revolution—the Western labor shortage, real and perceived—they also spring from other deep sources and questions, including what it means to be a nation and a citizen in a globalized world.

To name other forces ancillary but still salient to this book's thesis, globalization contributes to the crisis of identity too—in part because it also increases familial dislocation. So does the immediacy of the Internet, which throws gasoline on the burning question of identity in several ways: by showing the have-nots what the haves enjoy in a more up close and personal way than ever before, by handing the angry and discontented a new power of convening, by making solipsistic "silos" a go-to, and, above all, by delivering simulacrums of "groups" and "friends" to a world in which many postrevolutionary souls are already lacking the real-life version of both.

Even so, the simultaneous phenomena of globalization and the Internet amount to comorbidities under which another, deeper malady has already steadily depleted our species' immune system. What most ails great swaths of the country and the West today is something more fundamental than income disparity or a Gini coefficient, and more primordial than any digital act of bonding.

In sum, the fact of a multiplicity of influences on our politics and culture does not negate the truth that some are better understood than others. The fact that racism and sexism exist does not make the crackup of the Western family any less integral to the post-1960s human story. To argue by way of analogy, there are causes of lung cancer besides smoking tobacco, but that did not make the crusaders against tobacco in the twentieth century wrong in drawing attention to its dangers. There were other sources of child-hood harm during the Industrial Revolution besides exploitative employment, but that did not make the early Victorian reformers wrong to argue against, and eventually abolish, child labor.

Many voices, both supportive of and opposed to identity politics, have discussed what this new code of conduct within the polity is *doing to us*. This book asks a different question, which is what the nonstop obsession with identity is *telling us*—about ourselves, our society, our civilization, and how our radical new way of living is transforming all of the above. My purpose is not to excoriate identity politics, as other writers, left and right, already have. It is rather to put forward a new theory of why so many people seem to have lost their very selves, with the result that Western polities and societies now resound with languages of loss, fury, and rancor.

The question before us is not the political one, as in, *What are we to do about identity politics?* It is instead anthropological: *Why can't Narcissus stop looking for himself?*

PART ONE

PRIMAL SCREAMS

1

The Conversation So Far, and Its Limitations

In order to approach the "why" question, it is necessary, first, to take a step back in the conversation and ask a "what" question—as in, *what* points relevant to this book's thesis have been made about identity politics so far?

One early insight into the shifting sense of self appeared in a landmark work in which the phrase "identity politics," ironically, does not so much as make an appearance. With *The Closing of the American Mind*, first published in 1987, professor Allan Bloom of the University of Chicago produced a surprise best-seller.[1] Part moral diagnostic and part cri de coeur, *Closing* would go on to influence a generation of critics struggling to pin down what, exactly, had transformed the great quads of the academy into places where increasingly aggrieved factions were abjuring Western civilization itself.

Bloom's dissection was controversial then and remains so. For one thing, the professor's erudition all but ensured that many readers who would have empathized with his argument did not read it (as Friedrich Nietzsche quipped of Immanuel Kant, he wrote for the common man in language that only a scholar could understand).[2] For another, Bloom's critique of "vulgar" relativism in the academy was received frostily by many academics. Simultaneously, his extended attack on rock music, in particular, guaranteed that many readers, especially though not only on the left, would dismiss *Closing* as the midlife tantrum of a cultural reactionary.

But one need not sign on to all, or indeed any, of Bloom's other theses to find in his analysis of young souls an advance notice of what seemed to be a new rip in the human fabric. Citing Rousseau's *Emile*, in which the education of a student is undertaken "in the absence of any organic relation between husbands and wives and parents and children," as Bloom put it, *Closing* summarized the young as follows: "That is it. Everyone has 'his own little separate system.' The aptest description I can find for the state of students' souls is the psychology of separateness."[3]

What Bloom discerned was not identity politics per se, but the antecedent without which they would not have been possible: the unique isolation of the late Baby Boomers and Generation Xers who were populating his college classrooms. And though this aspect of his argument does not seem to have been much noticed, Bloom repeatedly connected the solitariness of his students to a phenomenon experienced by more and more: divorce. "The most visible sign of our increasing separateness," he argued, and "the cause of ever greater separateness, is divorce. It has a deep influence on our universities because more and more of the students are products of it, and they not only have problems themselves but also affect other students and the general atmosphere."[4]

Three decades ago, that is to say, a link between the country's devitalized homes and the aloneness of their emerging young residents was visible, at least to one perspicacious if perennially controversial professor.

The bridge between Bloom's observations and the identity politics to come arrived in the form of another word that did not appear as such in *Closing*: multiculturalism.

To some people, "multiculturalism" meant, and means, something as anodyne as the embrace of ideas and traditions different from our own. On campuses and elsewhere though, multiculturalism beginning in the 1980s came to mean something divergent and more virulent: the idea that all cultures have equal value—except for Western civilization, which has less.

Paradigmatic was the revolt on January 15, 1987, at Stanford University, during which some five hundred students led by the Rev. Jesse Jackson marched to the chant, "Hey hey, ho, ho, Western Civ has got to go." Two years later, its "Western Culture" introductory humanities program would be replaced with the "Culture, Ideas, and Values" program with its "more inclusive works on race, class, and gender," as Stanford's archive puts it.[5]

Whether all of those who sought a more "inclusive" curriculum simultaneously wanted to jettison the Western canon is unknowable in retrospect. But the emblematic political theater at Stanford captured a zero-sum thinking that persists to this day in discussions of identity politics: the idea that the tradition formed by Athens and Jerusalem, Christianity and Western philosophy, was the designated enemy of "diversity" in the eyes of multiculturalism's defenders.

What happened at Stanford didn't stay at Stanford. Resistance to multiculturalism soon became a rallying cry for conservativism, one that united libertarians and social conservatives as other issues did not. Also downstream of that same eruption came a number of new books in the 1990s and early 2000s, assessing what multiculturalism and its emerging sibling, identity politics, would mean for the making or unmaking of the United States. Of these, three delivered assessments of identity politics that were especially prescient regarding the conversation to come.

In *The Disuniting of America: Reflections on a Multicultural Society*, first published in 1992 and then enlarged and republished in 1998, Arthur M. Schlesinger Jr. sounded notes that rang through other critiques written years later: that the separatism of such politics "nourishes prejudices, magnifies differences, and stirs antagonisms," thereby undermining a common identity.[6]

Citing the Marxist historian Eric Hobsbawm, who argued that the political project of the left "should be for *all* human beings," Schlesinger also worried especially about multiculturalism's toxic effect on the left's traditionally universalist agenda. The "hurt-feelings standard," he charged, resulted in a "censorship strategy" that would, inter alia, "hand the free speech issue to the right"—a prophecy now enacted nightly on Fox News, among other venues where conservative voices routinely and correctly flag the stifling of expression out of keeping with progressive conformity, especially in the academy.

Vivid though his prognostications were, what leaps out most about Schlesinger's analysis in hindsight is that like Allan Bloom, he was troubled by what seemed to be an increasingly emotive, irrational tone in public life—especially among the young. Also like Bloom, he sought a root cause, ultimately identifying "world shrinkage"—what we would now call globalization—as the destroyer-in-chief. "The more people feel themselves adrift in a vast, impersonal, anonymous sea, the more desperately they swim toward any familiar, intelligible, protective life-raft; the more they crave a politics of identity," he observed.

Also ahead of his time, and also writing from the left in the 1990s, Todd Gitlin surveyed what he called *The Twilight of Common Dreams: Why America Is Wracked by Culture Wars.*[7] While disputing the conservative analyses as overheated and ill informed, Gitlin emphasized nonetheless that "the campaign against PC [political correctness]" resonated for one big reason: because "identity politics and attendant censoriousness were real."[8] The "triumph of identity politics," he wrote, meant "intellectual parochialism."[9]

Twilight is also useful as a gauge of how powerful identity politics has become in the years since. In 1995, one could still say to a liberal-left audience, as Gitlin did, that "the Enlightenment is not to be discarded because Voltaire was anti-Semitic or Hume, Kant, Hegel, and Jefferson racist . . . for it equips us with the tools with which to refute the anti-Semitism of a Voltaire and the racism of the others."[10] It is a measure of the ferocity—and success—of identity politics since then that those would be fighting words to many liberals and progressives today.

In 2012, cultural critic Bruce Bawer published a book that was also insightful, illustrating both the programmatic march of identity politics through the institutions and the increasing incoherence of its academic jargon. *The Victims' Revolution: The Rise of Identity Studies and the Closing of the Liberal Mind* explored the widespread rejection of classical learning and its supplanting by ideologies of identity throughout the academy.[11] It also delivered an inside account of the dramatic intellectual transformation from the 1970s through the 1990s—the same years, inter alia, during which the first generations born after the sexual revolution were coming of age.

The Victims' Revolution is especially compelling for zeroing in on the literary embarrassments of these new "identity studies"— the indecipherable prose committed in the names of "women's

studies," "black studies," "Aztlan theory," "male studies," "fat studies," and the rest of the catalog, ad infinitum. Consider the following incomprehensible example that appeared in the journal
Diacritics, authored by one of the pioneers of "queer theory":

> The move from a structuralist account in which capital
> is understood to structure social relations in relatively
> homologous ways to a view of hegemony in which power
> relations are subject to repetition, convergence, and
> rearticulation brought the question of temporality into
> the thinking of structure, and marked a shift from a form
> of Althusserian theory that takes structural totalities as
> theoretical objects to one in which the insights into the
> contingent possibility of structure inaugurate a renewed
> conception of hegemony as bound up with the contingent
> sites and strategies of the rearticulation of power.[12]

Yet the infelicity of the identitarian argot only raises the
question once more: why, for generations now, have so many
students—including the sort who are educated enough to attain
entry into the most elite colleges and universities—been falling for this patois in the first place? What, exactly, in this awful
cacophony is singing to them?

The next and most recent chapter in the developing conversation over identity politics began late in 2016. Just when it seemed
as if the election of Donald Trump had rendered his support-
ers incoherent with triumphalism and his detractors incoherent
with rage—thereby dumbing down political conversation for a
long time to come—something different and more interesting happened. A genuine debate sprang up among liberals and

progressives not only in the United States, but in other countries grappling with the same subject: identity politics.

Jump-started by a manifesto called *The Once and Future Liberal: After Identity Politics*, by Columbia University professor and liberal Mark Lilla, the ensuing discussion revealed even more clearly than before the struggles within the American left between the defenders and detractors of identity-first thinking. The purpose of Lilla's broadside was twofold: first, to denounce identity politics, sometimes called "identity liberalism," and second, to convince his "fellow liberals that their current way of looking at the country, speaking to it, teaching the young, and engaging in practical politics has been misguided and counterproductive."

As the *Stanford Encyclopedia of Philosophy* explains in its entry on the subject, "Wherever they line up in the debates, thinkers agree that the notion of identity has become indispensable to contemporary political discourse."[13] Like Schlesinger, Gitlin, and other critics on the liberal-left before him, the author of *The Once and Future Liberal* offered an explanation for the resort to such politics. "Thirty years of economic growth and technological advance that followed the Second World War," he argued, combined with new geographic, institutional, and erotic mobility, have led to a "hyperindividualistic bourgeois society, materially and in our cultural dogmas." Flush with prosperity and unprecedented new freedoms, we moderns went on to atomize ourselves: "*Personal* choice. *Individual* rights. *Self*-definition. We speak these words as if a wedding vow." By the 1980s, such hyperindividualism coalesced into a "Reagan dispensation," which prized self-reliance and small government over the collective—thus marking a radical break from the preceding "Roosevelt dispensation," emphasizing more communal attachments, including duty and solidarity with one another.

By embracing the politics of identity, this professor argued, liberals and progressives had unwittingly contaminated their politics with "Reaganism for lefties," resulting in the toxic consequences visible today: shutdowns of free speech on campuses, out-of-touch urban and globalized elites, and a political nonorder deformed into a "victimhood Olympics."

In effect, Mark Lilla's was a supply-side answer to the "why" question: identity politics became the order of the day *because it could*. That is, on the surface, an unassailable claim. But missing from that analysis—as from other analyses of identity politics, right as well as left—is the demand-side answer to the same question: why have so many people found in such politics the very center of their political being?

After all: that identitarianism is now the heart and soul of politics itself for many people, not only in America but elsewhere, is a visceral truth—as visceral as the footage of campus turmoil now seen with a frequency that would have shocked most citizens only a decade ago. What's singular about such politics, many would say, is exactly its profound and immediate emotivism, its frightening volatility, its instantaneous ignition into unreasoned violence. The author of *The Once and Future Liberal* acknowledged this reality indirectly in describing "a kind of moral panic about racial, gender and sexual identity"—all true, as far as it goes. But the problem is that reality is far less nuanced.

When a mob of young men attack a seventy-four-year-old man and a middle-aged woman, sending the latter to the emergency room with significant injuries—as happened at Middlebury College in 2017, in the case of visiting speaker Charles Murray and Allison Stranger—something deeper is afoot than American individualism run amok.[14] When debate after debate is preemptively shut down due to threats of violence on social media—as happened at Oxford University in 2014, among other examples, when a scheduled debate over abortion was shuffled around and finally cancelled—talk of a Reagan dispensation doesn't begin to capture the menace there.[15] And consider these: $100,000 in damages from a riot over a 2017 appearance by provocateur Milo Yiannopolos at University of California, Berkeley;[16] $600,000 spent in "security" on the same campus upon a visit by conservative Ben Shapiro;[17] increasing demands by administrations that student groups inviting unpopular speakers fork over unexpected high sums, again in the name of "security." To ascribe these and related transgressions to overheated individualism is to miss what's truly novel about them. And frightening.

Contra Mark Lilla's otherwise compelling critique, what's happening on campuses and elsewhere today is not merely "a pseudo-politics of self-regard." It's all panic, all the time, served up with more than a smidgeon of violence. Even the phrasing "assaults on free speech" does not suffice to capture the gravity of the new menace—though of course these occurrences are that too.[18] The point is that many of today's protests are not your grandmother's 1960s political protests at all. Often, they are exercises in dangerous collective hysteria, as more and more observers and firsthand participants now testify.

Writing after a 2015 lecture at Oberlin College on feminism that was mocked, jeered, and peopled by protestors whose mouths were covered in duct tape, for example, Christina Hoff Sommers commented on the "cult-like" behavior witnessed there.[19] Charles Murray reported similarly of the attack at Middlebury College that he had never encountered anything like the irrationality and ferocity seen that day.[20] Heather Mac Donald described a harrowing two days spent on different quads in California in 2017.[21] The subject of her scheduled speech—the importance of adequate policing in the crime-plagued inner cities—tripped ideological alarms. As a result, at Claremont McKenna College, a mob of two hundred aided by megaphones and amplifiers prevented people from entering the hall; nervous administrators first moved her podium away from a window, then escorted her to a safe house via an unmarked police car. What she did manage to deliver of her talk was accompanied by chants, shrieks, drums, and poundings on the walls outside.[22] At University of California, Los Angeles, following another speech on the same trip, screaming protestors stormed the event, and she had to be removed with a police escort.[23]

This raw aggression, repeated on campus after campus and elsewhere, goes missing from liberal-left examinations of identity politics. It is also characteristically underplayed in right-conservative accounts as well, which tend to focus on the *principle* of free speech, as opposed to the *practice* of mass hysteria. It is true, as Mark Lilla observed, that the exercise of identity politics encourages people to "descend into the rabbit hole of self." But the question remains: what deep gravitational force keeps pulling so many toward that hole in the first place?

In a widely discussed essay published in the *Atlantic* in 2015, "The Coddling of the American Mind," later expanded to an eponymous book, Greg Lukianoff and Jonathan Haidt took a closer look at the precarious mental dimension of identity politics.[24]

"Something strange is happening at American colleges and universities," they reported, and "some of the actions [on campus] border on surreal." The authors dubbed the phenomenon "vindictive protectiveness"—a runaway effort to protect students from psychological harm, including by punishing putative transgressors.

Alarmed by this development for several reasons—not least because it might teach students to think "pathologically"—Haidt and Lukianoff also pointed to empirical measures of collegiate psychic disintegration. Most arresting, they noted:

> Rates of mental illness in young adults have been rising, both on campus and off, in recent decades. . . . [And] most experts seem to agree that some portion of the trend is real. *Nearly all of the campus mental-health directors surveyed in 2013 by the American College Counseling Association reported that the number of students with severe psychological problems was rising at their schools* [emphasis added].

The authors also pointed to another red flag reported earlier and elsewhere by others, including former Berkeley psychiatrist Miriam Grossman in her pathbreaking 2007 book *Unprotected: A Campus Psychiatrist Reveals How Political Correctness in Her Profession Endangers Every Student*: that self-reported emotional distress on campus has been rising higher and higher.[25]

These analyses are of a piece with what is now a substantial body of work indicating that the psychological state of young America, in particular, looks rockier than has ever been recorded before. Another source is psychologist Jean Twenge, whose research documenting the increase in mental fragility among today's young appears in her books *Generation Me* (2006) and *The Narcissism Epidemic* (2010).[26] In the latter, she and coauthor W. Keith Campbell report that data from 37,000 college students have shown that narcissistic personality traits were rising as fast as obesity rates, especially among women.[27] They further pinpointed the beginning of the narcissism explosion in the 1970s—a thesis that signals the uncanny foresight of Christopher Lasch, whose book *The Culture of Narcissism* heralded the epidemic's inception fully four decades ago.[28]

Also consistent with the data, people in their twenties and thirties are much more likely to turn to therapists than were earlier cohorts. "Millennials Are the Therapy Generation," as one 2019 report put it. Among other findings, this one relayed that "[according to] data from 147 colleges and universities, the number of students seeking mental-health help increased from 2011 to 2016 at five times the rate of new students starting college"; and a 2018 report from the Blue Cross Blue Shield Association found a 47 percent increase in those seeking mental health assistance between 2013 and 2016.[29]

Such systemwide descent into psychiatric trouble, extending over several decades, obviously calls for explanation. Haidt and Lukianoff zeroed in on three possibilities, none of them exclusive: heightened security and anxiety in schools following the mass shooting at Columbine High School, Colorado, in 1999; rising crime before the drop-off in the 1990s; and, of course, social media.

To amplify a note sounded in the introduction, there's no doubt that social media play a symbiotic role in the hyperdrama over identity. In "The Joy of Destruction," a piercing essay published in 2017 about the uniquely incendiary power of existence online, Joseph Bottum analyzed in depth the twisted effects of electronic identities.[30] Telling the story of one particular Antifa protestor arrested in Charlottesville ("Josh"), and how he went from computer screen to jail in a few easy steps, Bottum pointed out that Josh's tale, like that of many other contemporary radicals, would have been unimaginable before the age of cyberspace. As he summarized the dynamic, "The mildly supportive become strongly supportive, the strongly supportive become wildly supportive, and the wildly supportive become fanatical psychopaths."

Yet for all that public life and private life alike are being configured and disfigured by connectivity, even social media and the

Internet do not answer the "why" question about identity frenzy. They beg it, for two reasons: first, because identity politics predates the Internet itself; second, because the narcissism of social media just raises the question all over again. Why has finding ourselves in cyberspace become a major avocation for so very many people?

Other writers have offered a different explanation for the fury behind identity politics: "white racism," or, as the current term of art prefers it, "whiteness."

In a piece titled "America's First White President," published shortly after the 2016 election, *Salon* executive editor Andrew O'Hehir delivered a prototype of this line of thought. "Trump," he wrote, "is the first president defined by whiteness, the first whose glaring and overwhelming whiteness is a salient issue that lies at the core of his appeal"; the "presidential candidate's race played a central role in his campaign, and is one of the key factors that got him elected"; and the election result amounted to retribution of some kind for America's having formerly, twice, elected a black president ("the election of Barack Obama inflicted a psychic wound that demanded immediate payback, at almost any cost").[31]

In an essay published in 2017, similarly called "The First White President," Ta-Nehisi Coates made a related case: "To Trump, whiteness is neither notional nor symbolic but is the very core of his power"; Trump "is a white man who would not be president were it not for this fact"; and Trump is "the first president whose entire political existence hinges on the fact of a black president."[32] This essay also included an attack on several other high-profile writers of the left as unworthy and/or unreliable commentators on identity politics—on the grounds that "those charged with analyzing him [Trump] cannot name his essential nature, because they too are implicated in it." [33]

As such essays went to show, alongside a great deal of other commentary, the idea that white racism is the root of today's identity politics is widely shared among progressives. Once again, though, as an explanation for the ubiquity of the new-found Western preoccupation with identity, white racism doesn't suffice—for the simple reason that so many other members in the identitarian coalition claim different motivations, different oppressors, and different grievances.

Perhaps most notable of all are the identity-firsters of sexual politics, whose influence on law and culture has been prodigious during the past quarter century. In addition to the epiphenome-nal manifestations of the obsession over sexual and gender iden-tity—Facebook's seventy-one genders, media focus on intersex and transgender people, "bathroom wars," and the rest—there are also the areas into which sexual identitarianism has sunk last-ing roots.

For example, ten countries now allow for identification as something other than male or female,[34] and a growing number of states and other authorities leave gender identity in various forms to personal say-so.[35] Marriage, adoption, and other areas of family law have been reconfigured around the world. In fact, viewing the whole of identity politics through the single lens of public efficacy, one would have to say that sexual identitarians have both exercised and obtained more power than any other single group in the coalition. Whiteness and racism do not explain their exis-tence either.

As various high-profile cases have shown, such as Senator Elizabeth Warren's apology to a leader of the Cherokee Nation for taking a DNA test revealing that her vaunted Native American ancestry was minute, it can be problematic to believe, as many identity-firsters now claim, that "I am whatever, and whoever, I say I am."[36] Critics have naturally objected to such an implied repudiation of empirical reality; understandably, some have mocked it. But our purpose here, once more, is to do something else: listen and learn. In the insistence that the human animal is free to rewrite everything about himself, including his origins and sex, we see once more that the question *Who am I?* is the preeminent psychic howl of our time.

White racism explains many terrible events, and as noted at the outset, it is a major reason why some people in racial minority groups are drawn to identitarianism in the first place: for reasons of collective protection. But whiteness does not—and cannot—explain the primordial emotionalism and fierce irrationality that have come to be part and parcel of *all* identity-first expression.

There is also, and finally, the most popular theme now making the rounds about identity politics, one which illuminates best of all the shortcomings of previous interpretations. That is the notion that current politics is best understood as a species of "tribalism."

The torrent of commentary centered on the "tribes" metaphor is now so omnipresent as to defy easy summary. Thus, to name just a few examples, in *The Red and the Blue: The 1990s and the Birth of Political Tribalism*, Steve Kornacki traced today's divide to the political battles between Bill Clinton and Newt Gingrich.[37] In an essay on "tribes in the age of Trump," also appearing in fall 2018, George Packer dated what he likewise called "tribalism" to the same origin.[38] Andrew Sullivan and many other writers have said similarly that the United States is engaged in a war between "two tribes."[39] And so on, ad infinitum. "Tribalism" has become the it-word of political punditry.

All of which brings us to the question left unanswered by that talk of "tribalism": what, exactly, has caused so many Americans to find their very selves in such associations in the first place?

Sullivan, like others, advanced a list of "accelerants" from across the past few decades: the failed nomination of Judge Robert Bork, mass illegal Latino immigration, Newt Gingrich, talk radio, Fox News, Internet and MSNBC news, partisan gerrymandering, absence of compulsory military service, multiculturalism, declining Christianity, rural "brain drain," and more. No doubt, taken together, these disparate events explain *something* about the political trajectory that led to identity politics.

But does one really become part of a horde, defined in opposition to other hordes, over quotidian prompts like these? Doesn't the very word "tribal" suggest that something more primal may be in the mix too?

The answer can only be *of course*. A real tribe is no more a band of unrelated pack travelers than the imaginary wolf pack. And just as the tribe is antecedent to the state, something else is antecedent to the tribe—something missing from all the high-profile talk, pro and con, about how and why societies have become riddled with identity politics.

In laying out the particulars of today's tribes, for example, Sullivan writes "of unconditional pride, in our neighborhood and community; in our ethnic and social identities and their rituals; among our fellow enthusiasts. There are hip-hop and country-music tribes; bros; nerds; Wasps; Dead Heads and Packers fans; Facebook groups. . . . And then, most critically, there is the *Über*-tribe that constitutes the nation-state, a megatribe that unites a country around shared national rituals, symbols, music, history, mythology, and events."

This is a key passage not only as an example of "tribe-think," but also in the wider, and widening, argument of this book—because it omits what is, or once was, the alpha tribe of all. It is not the case that "America Wasn't Built for Humans," as the title on Sullivan's *New York* piece put the point. It is rather that America, like other civilizations, was built for humans who learned community not from roving bands of unrelated nomads, but from those around them—beginning in the smallest and first community of all, the family. [40]

In book III, chapter 8 of *Democracy in America*, Alexis de Tocqueville writes of how democratic governance shapes familial relations, rendering fathers and sons more equal and closer and less hierarchical than their aristocratic counterparts. If it was and remains obvious that a given form of government can shape the family, isn't it even more obvious that the first polity to which future citizens belong—the family—will shape the kind of citizens they become?

This, finally, is the insurmountable problem with the "tribes" metaphor: its faulty anthropology. Tribes themselves grow out of units of family and extended family. Humanity does not gravitate toward anonymous or "forced" packs any more than our fellow creatures do. To believe otherwise is to accept a just-so story that doesn't hold up under inspection, like the fable of the lone wolf. And though current commentary has overlooked it, the familial dimension of individual identity has been acknowledged and explored by diverse thinkers, including during the past half century.

One is the aforementioned Christopher Lasch, who in addition to *The Culture of Narcissism* was known for decades as the left's most compelling defender of the traditional family against (what he argued were) capitalism's transgressions.[41] Another is psychologist and psychoanalyst Erik Erikson, who coined the phrase "identity crisis" itself in the course of treating traumatized former soldiers. He too emphasized the influence of family on personality development. Observing that humans have the longest "biological childhood," for example, Erikson argued that childhood and adolescence were the crucibles of the self "because man must have time to learn: all his high specialization and all his intricate capabilities of co-ordination and reflection are, in fact, contingent upon his prolonged dependence"[42]—a point to which we will return in chapter 6, especially.

These examples of forgotten literature bring us to the most unnoticed explanation of all concerning why so many postrevolutionary people these days are scrambling to figure out who they are.

2

A New Theory

Our macropolitics have become a mania about identity, because our micropolitics are no longer familial: this, above all, is what's happened during the decades in which identity politics went from being a phrase in an obscure quasiradical document to a way of being that has gone on to transform academia, law, media, culture, and government. Maybe many people today are claiming to be victims because they and their societies *are* victims—not so much of the "isms" they point to as oppressors, but because the human animal has been selected for familial forms of socialization *that for many people no longer exist*.

In this chapter and those to follow, I'll expand and test this new theory of the Great Scattering via an array of evidence from social science, history, anthropology, and current events.

Up until the middle of the twentieth century, and barring the frequent foreshortening of life by disease or natural catastrophe, human expectations remained largely the same throughout the ages: that one would grow up to have children and a family; that parents and siblings and extended family would remain one's primal community; that, again barring the unforeseen, one would *have* parents and siblings and extended family in the first place; and that, conversely, it was a tragedy *not* to be part of a family.

The post-1960s order of sexual consumerism has upended every one of these expectations. It has erased the givenness into which generations are born. *Who am I?* is a universal human question. It becomes harder to answer if other basic questions are problematic or out of reach. *Who is my brother? Who is my father? Where, if anywhere, are my cousins, grandparents, nieces, nephews, and the rest of the organic connections through which humanity up until now channeled everyday existence?*

It is this loss of givenness that drives the frenzied search for identity these days, whether in the secular scholasticism concerning how to speak about ethnicity or in the belligerent fights over "cultural appropriation." Such phenomena are indeed bizarre, if we examine them with the instruments of Aristotelian logic. But if instead we understand them against the existential reality of today—one in which the human family has imploded, and in which many people, no matter how privileged otherwise, have been deprived of the most elementary of human connections— we can grasp in full why identity politics is the headline that just won't go away.

Who am I? An illiterate peasant of the Middle Ages was better equipped to answer that question than many people in advanced societies in this century. He may only have lived until age thirty— but he spent his days among family and in towns, practicing a shared faith, and thus developed a vivid sense of those to whom he was elementally connected, not just in the course of his life but before birth and after death.

Every one of the assumptions he could take for granted is now negotiable. No wonder erotic leanings and ethnic claims have become substitute answers to that eternal question, *Who am I?* Many people, especially younger people, now experience the likes of these as the *only* reliable answers to that question of identity—or at least, as answers that seem less ambiguous and laden than those that refer back to their family, or families, or lack thereof.

Consider as one form of proof the historical timeline.

To quote the *Stanford Encyclopedia of Philosophy* once more, "although 'identity politics' can draw on intellectual precursors from Mary Wollstonecraft to Frantz Fanon, writing that actually uses this specific phrase, with all its contemporary baggage, is limited almost exclusively to the last thirty years." At the beginning of that time period, historians agree, came the founding document of identity politics itself: "The Combahee River Collective Statement," a declaration that grew out of several years of meetings among black feminists in Massachusetts.

The key assertion of this manifesto, which prefigures the politics to come, is that "this focus on our own oppression is embodied in the concept of identity politics. We believe that the most profound and potentially most radical politics come directly out of our own identity, as opposed to working to end someone else's oppression."

And who is the "someone else" to whom the document refers? Men. "Contemporary Black feminism," the authors explain, "is the outgrowth of countless generations of personal sacrifice, militancy, and work by *our mothers and sisters* [emphasis added]." When men are mentioned in the Combahee document, it is largely as adversaries with "habitually sexist ways of interacting with and oppressing Black women." Similarly: "The reaction of Black men to feminism has been notoriously negative. They are, of course, even more threatened than Black women by the possibility that Black feminists might organize around our own needs."

The founding document of identity politics, in other words, reflects aspects of the world as many African American women would have found it in the 1970s—and they had become the canaries in the coal mines of the revolution. Ahead of other groups, they were early witnesses to the transformations that are now the stuff of daily conversation and reality for all: a world in which men have become ever less trustworthy and reliable, in which relations between the sexes have become chronically estranged and consumerist, and in which marriage has become thin on the ground. African American women were—and still are—disproportionately affected by abortion, out-of-wedlock births, fatherless homes, and related metrics.

Is it really any wonder that the first collective articulation of identity politics comes from a community where familial identity was becoming increasingly riven from the very dawn of the revolution—a harbinger of what would come next for everyone else?

Consider as more suggestive evidence this bit of arithmetic.

The year of the document's publication—1977—was a watershed of a sort. The preceding year, the out-of-wedlock birth rate for black Americans had just "tipped" over the 50 percent mark. This rate kept climbing to its current high of 70-plus percent in 2016. At the same time, other measures indicating the splintering of the nuclear and extended family expanded too. By 2012, Millennials—women who were then under the age of thirty—shared for the first time the out-of-wedlock birth rate of black women in 1977 (i.e., over half). Millennials, of course, are the demographic backbone of identity politics.

Just how attenuated have family ties become? Let us count up a few of the ways.

GONE DADDY

When sociologists first began mapping the postrevolutionary empirical world beginning a little over half a century ago, they looked first, naturally enough, to the terrain that was easiest to see and measure. Fatherlessness and its correlates were among those.

In his famous and infamous report published in 1965, *The Negro Family: The Case for National Action*, future senator Daniel Patrick Moynihan argued that black poverty was tied fundamentally to the implosion of the black family, and worried over the rate of out-of-wedlock births—which was then around 25 percent, much higher than that of whites. That rate would continue to rise for both whites and blacks during the decades to come. In the pages of journals like the *Public Interest*, as well as in academic venues, sociologists and other specialists began connecting dots to show what was happening to children and adolescents in the new social order.[1]

In 1997, one of the most eminent social scientists of the twentieth century, James Q. Wilson, summarized many of these findings succinctly in a speech that was later published as an essay.[2] He identified the root of America's fracturing in the dissolution of the family. Wilson—professor of government at Harvard, professor emeritus at University of California, Los Angeles, and a former head of the American Political Science Association—described what he called "the two nations" of America.

The image of two nations, Wilson explained, harked back to an 1845 novel by Benjamin Disraeli, the future prime minister of

Great Britain. These were the separate, nonintersecting worlds of rich and poor. Between these two nations, Disraeli described, there was "no intercourse and no sympathy"—they were "as ignorant of each other's habits, thoughts, and feelings, as if they were . . . inhabitants of different planets."

More than a century and a half later, Wilson argued, the United States had also become two nations, but the dividing line was no longer one of income or social class. Instead, it had become all about the hearth. "It is not money," he observed, "but the family that is the foundation of public life. As it has become weaker, every structure built upon that foundation has become weaker." By 1997, family dissolution in America was no longer a phenomenon of the ghetto, but a fact of everyday life for more and more of the country.

Wilson pointed to the library that social science had been building for decades, filled with books and studies about the correlations between fatherlessness, especially, and various behavioral outcomes. Family structure had become more important to positive outcomes than race, income, or one's station at birth:

> Children in one-parent families, compared to those in two-parent ones, are twice as likely to drop out of school. Boys in one-parent families are much more likely than those in two-parent ones to be both out of school and out of work. Girls in one-parent families are twice as likely as those in two-parent ones to have an out-of-wedlock birth. These differences are not explained by income. . . . Children raised in single-parent homes [are] more likely to be suspended from school, to have emotional problems, and to behave badly.

As Wilson's summary went to show, the sociological data assembled since the 1960s has been overwhelming—all of it proving that the metamorphosis of the family was also transforming politics and society. Two-plus decades and many more books and scholars and research studies later, a whole new wing has been added to that same library. It underscores Wilson's point: the new wealth in America is familial wealth, and the new poverty, familial poverty.

At the same time, absent fathers have been only the most visible and measurable of the new family lacunae.

GONE CHILD

In a landmark 2000 book called *Between Two Worlds: The Inner Lives of Children of Divorce*, Elizabeth Marquardt, working with sociologist Norval Glenn, conducted the first study into the long-term effects of parental breakup into adulthood. She administered a lengthy questionnaire to fifteen hundred young adults, half of whose parents had split up by the time the children turned fourteen. Marquardt documented differences between the children whose parents had divorced and those who came from intact families—differences on issues including trust, anxiety, spirituality, and other broad measures.

For the purposes of this work, what stands out are several questions revealing another difference between the groups: at times, they exhibit starkly opposed concepts of *identity*.

For example, children of divorce were almost three times as likely to "strongly agree" with the statement, "I felt like a different person with each of my parents." They were also twice as likely to "strongly agree" with the statement, "I always felt like an adult, even when I was a little kid"—a particularly poignant expression of confusion about the question *Who am I?* Almost two-thirds of the respondents of divorced homes also "agreed" with the following statement, which similarly expresses the division of one self into more than one: "I felt like I had two families."[3]

This is evocative evidence, again, of the deeply changed sense of self that many people, adult and child alike, now experience as the givens of life. It expresses the division of one into more than one—of selves torn, as in the book's title, between worlds. And though these researchers limited their study to children of divorce only, their findings would also appear to apply to homes where parents never married, yet where both continue to play a role in the child's life from different locations.

Given the circumstances through which more and more of us enter society in the first place, the question is no longer whether primordial scars might have something to do with the palpable anxiety over identity. The question is rather, *how could they not?*

Compelling though it is, social science isn't the only way of affirming that broken homes have been raising fundamental questions of identity for a long time now.

In a 2004 essay called "Eminem Is Right" published in *Policy Review*, I documented something that seemed—and still seems—a seminal fact: that family rupture, family anarchy, and family breakup had become the signature themes of Generation-X and Generation-Y pop.

> If yesterday's rock was the music of abandon, today's is that of abandon*ment*. The odd truth about contemporary teenage music—the characteristic that most separates it from what has gone before—is its compulsive insistence on the damage wrought by broken homes, family dysfunction, checked-out parents, and (especially) absent fathers. Papa Roach, Everclear, Blink-182, Good Charlotte, Eddie Vedder and Pearl Jam, Kurt Cobain and Nirvana, Tupac

Shakur, Snoop Doggy Dogg, Eminem—these and other singers and bands, all of them award-winning top-40 performers who either are or were among the most popular icons in America, have their own generational answer to what ails the modern teenager. Surprising though it may be to some, that answer is: dysfunctional childhood. . . .

To put this perhaps unexpected point more broadly, during the same years in which progressive-minded and politically correct adults have been excoriating Ozzie and Harriet as artifacts of 1950s-style oppression, many millions of American teenagers have enshrined a new generation of music idols whose shared signature in song after song is to rage about what *not* having had a nuclear family has done to them.[4]

In 2004, identity politics was not the omnipresent headline it is today. Even so, the effect of family decline on the sense of oneself was already being writ large across popular music.

There is, for example, the confusion of not knowing whether one is parent or child, expressed as anger at parents for not being parents. Tupac Shakur, one case in point, rapped about life with a single mother and no male parent, including in a 1993 offering, "Papa'z Song," dominated by the image of a boy who has to play catch by himself. Many other pop songs from those years and beyond express longing for another, better life—one might say: another, better identity. In the ironically named "Wonderful," a 2000 rock ballad about divorce by the band Everclear, the narrator sings of going to his room and pretending to be somewhere else—somewhere new. Eddie Vedder of Pearl Jam and Kurt Cobain of Nirvana, both towering figures in 1990s rock, were also children of divorce, and both referred back to that seminal event repeatedly in their songs and interviews.

The themes of split identity and divided hearts mentioned by subjects in the Marquardt study on divorce appear regularly in post-sexual-revolution rock and rap. Papa Roach's 2000 "Broken Home," another song about parental breakup, is a raw tale of depression, substance abuse, and violence delivered by a narrator wishing he were somewhere else. Singer Pink's breakthrough 2001 album, *Missundaztood*, revolved entirely around her parents' split; its lyrics include references to not wanting two addresses, or two places to go on holidays—or stepsiblings. In all of these examples and others, parental loss is interpreted as corrosive to the sense of one's self.

In the song "Family Portrait," Pink also mentioned not wanting her mother to take a new name. Names, and the act of naming—obvious markers of identity—are features of this same musical landscape. In the chorus to "Father of Mine" (1997), Art Alexakis of Everclear reiterated his anguish over the fact that his father named him, and then left. Another popular band of the 1990s, Good Charlotte, included twin brothers whose parents' divorce looms large in numerous songs. In a symbolically charged move, both legally changed their last name to their mother's maiden name as a vote of protest against their father.[5]

Above all, there is the fiery emotional connection that generations of teenagers have found in bad boy rap superstar Eminem. It exists not only on account of his extraordinary facility with language, but also, surely, for his signature themes: absent father, inattentive mother, protectiveness toward a sibling, and rage. Eminem is the Greek chorus of family dysfunction.

Long before today's bizarre panics on campuses and markedly coarser politics, a lot of young America was already stumbling over how to answer the question *Who am I?* Just listening to what they were driving up the charts proved the point.

GONE PARENT

Another round of evidence about the connections between today's identity panic and the Great Scattering come from a new kind of identity erasure now underway: assisted reproduction technology, including such methods as anonymous sperm donation and surrogate pregnancy.

The creation of human beings purposefully deprived of knowing at least one, and sometimes both, genetic parents is an experiment so novel that it has yet to receive widespread scholarly attention. As well, the research territory is intrinsically complicated. No one knows how many children have come into existence through these techniques, which are largely unregulated in the United States. The fact that the industry spans other nations where data also go untracked makes definitive information even harder to come by.

Still, the first major analysis of these techniques' effects on identity is suggestive in the extreme. In a 2010 study *My Daddy's Name Is Donor: A New Study of Young Adults Conceived through Sperm Donation*, Elizabeth Marquardt, Norval D. Glenn, and Karen Clark assembled the first representative sample of 485 adults between the ages of eighteen and forty-five whose mother had used a sperm donor and compared their survey results with those from a group of 563 adults who had been raised by their biological parents.[6] "On average," the authors report, "young adults conceived through sperm donation are hurting more, are more confused, and feel more isolated from their families. They fare worse than their peers raised by biological parents on important outcomes such as depression, delinquency and substance abuse."

In addition to such outcomes, which track with those of the fatherless home in general, there are clear signs of identity confusion. About two-thirds of the sample, for example, agreed with the statement, "My sperm donor is half of who I am." That is half a self left hanging in limbo. But the singular stresses of the donor-conceived are not limited to the most obvious problem of hunger for a missing parent. The survey results also yield this eye-opener:

> More than half say that when they see someone who resembles them they wonder if they are related. Almost as many say they have feared being attracted to or having sexual relations with someone to whom they are unknowingly related.

It is hard to think of a more fundamental marker for human identity than the incest taboo—the establishment of who, exactly, is an acceptable or forbidden possible mate. People who cannot navigate by that marker are people who cannot easily answer *Who am I?* at its most basic level. Small wonder, then, that the children of the anonymous have come to renorm as a kind of human "forced pack." As the *Atlantic* has reported, the rise of consumer DNA testing means that such former children now have access to information about donors and half siblings never available before—information that "can change who they believe themselves to be and, in some sense, *who they are* [emphasis added]."[7]

The children of sperm donation are small in numbers relative to the rest of the population; Marquardt and her colleagues in their report estimate that between thirty thousand and sixty thousand such babies are born in the United States each year, a tiny fraction of births overall. But the mapping of their emotional state renders a truth that applies across the spectrum for all of us: human beings try to answer the question *Who am I?* by knowing who their relations are—even when they have been deprived of that knowledge on purpose. *Relatedness* is the tool of first resort for constructing identity, which is why the donor children take it up to find themselves. This social experiment proves, however inadvertently, that human beings resist genealogical obliteration—one is tempted to say, instinctively.

My Daddy's Name Is Donor also reports that "about half of donor offspring have concerns about or serious objections to donor conception itself, even when parents tell their children the truth." That so many people object to their own origins—to *who they are*—is one more example, however unusual, of showing that sense of self and sense of one's own are joined at the root.

GONE SIBLINGS

Another demographic contender of note is the numerical shrinkage of most Western families, whether split or intact—one of whose consequences is the diminishing number of people who grow up with siblings.

The reasons for imploding family size are many. In addition to divorce and the rise in single-parent homes, both of which render large families less manageable, there is also the fact that older motherhood and late marriage tend to make families of size less likely for reasons of biology. As well, other social and financial pressures lean in the direction of smaller families: job insecurity, student loan debt, continuing education, career growth, caring for elderly parents, a desire to maximize freedom, and as of late, worries over contributing to climate change.[8]

As a result of these changing pressures and preferences, it is now much more common for American mothers to have one or two children, rather than three or more as was the case in the early 1960s. Singleton children have become the norm across much of Europe and parts of Asia, and the numbers are increasing in the United States. As the Pew Research Center notes, there is even talk of middle children going "extinct."[9]

Even so, there remains apposite literature about the efficacy of sibling bonds. For many years, psychologists and others investigating the effect of brothers and sisters on one another have reached similar conclusions. One—often cited in favor of the singleton home—is that only children are more likely to excel in school. This is a consistent finding that researchers commonsensically attribute to the greater resources that a parent or parents can devote to one, rather than multiple, children.

The second set of findings is the one germane to my purposes here, because it points toward the question of who learns identity more easily, and how. These results concern the role of siblings in child and adolescent socialization.

As we will see later on in chapter 6, part of the argument here is that the Great Scattering has also resulted in massive breakdowns of something that is a lifeline among all animals: social communication. Research on siblings takes us to what may be ground zero of that breakdown. Many contemporary children and adolescents not only lack a parent, typically a male parent, but many also have no siblings, or no sibling of the same or opposite sex.

Why might this matter? Because diverse findings show that being accompanied through early life by nonparental contemporaneous others (i.e., siblings) gives children and teenagers a leg up on socialization. On reflection, it is hard to see how things could be otherwise; after all, many siblings spend more time with one another than with parents, and the sibling relationship is the only familial relationship potentially capable of enduring across all or most of one's life.

One 1982 collection of sibling studies called *Sibling*

Relationships: Their Nature and Significance Across the Lifespan sum-marized the knowledge to date thus:

> Modern Western societies seldom assign specific roles in the socialization process to siblings. Wittingly or unwit-tingly, however, the evidence suggests that their influence is often profound. Siblings set and maintain standards, provide models to emulate and advice to consider, enact complementary roles in relation to one another through which both develop and practice social-interactional skills, and serve as confidantes and sources of nonjudg-mental social support in times of emotional stress.[10]

A Canadian study published in 2018 suggests that siblings also learn empathy from one another, independent of birth order.[11] Another study has found that the likelihood of divorce later in life can be predicted by the number of siblings one has; the higher that number, the lower the likelihood of divorce.[12] As in other analyses of the benefits of having brothers and sisters, this one conjectures that the necessity of sharing resources prepares sib-lings for essential social skills later in life, such as bargaining and taking turns. Siblings would also appear to be at least potentially protective against the scourge of loneliness.

Such findings are also suggestively consonant with similar observations made from inquiries into animal behavior. One paper reviewing research into a variety of primates, including rhesus monkeys, baboons, and macaques, makes the same point to emerge from the studies of humans:

> The bulk of the available evidence suggests that during childhood the nonhuman primates who grow up in the

presence of siblings (or maternal half-sibs) will develop childhood social relationships with others in their social group earlier; and that these relationships will be of a more extensive nature than those formed by infants who grow up in the absence of siblings (or maternal half-sibs).[13]

Observations about the social benefits of siblings do not amount to crude cultural arithmetic according to which the advantages rise ad infinitum with each additional brother or sister. But they point to phenomena too new for social science to have taken up as yet, which are the long- and short-term effects of having fewer people around to call one's own—like siblings. The same is true, by extension, for the disappearance of cousins, second cousins, aunts, uncles, and so on. Many postrevolutionary people already have fewer of *all* of the above than their predecessors—and given the ongoing reductions in family size, the generations ahead will have fewer still.

Other research has indicated the specific social benefits conveyed by having a sibling of the opposite sex. One study that made headlines recently showed with data what many might once have regarded as common sense: growing up with an opposite-sex sibling makes teenagers and young adults more confident and successful in the romance market, because they have had the opportunity to observe at close range a contemporaneous member of the opposite sex and have had the attendant prolonged experience of interacting with such a person in real life.[14]

This raises one more question to be taken up later on, which is whether the diminishing number of siblings might have wider effects after children leave the ancestral home. As one of the editors of *Sibling Relationships* also notes:

Besides marital relationships, sibling relationships are

often the only heterosexual relationships in which western adults can express affection and closeness without eliciting disapprobation and gossip. Heterosexual sibling relationships may be especially important in adolescence and early adulthood, when long-term sexual commitments are commonly explored for the first time.

GONE FAMILY

Another body of evidence that also speaks to our unique dislocation and isolation can be found in one of sociology's hottest and fastest-growing stocks: loneliness studies. These reveal profoundly disturbing data showing what the golden years are now like for many in the post-1960s West.

Substantial numbers of men and women are suffering from what social scientists and medical professionals in their stricken societies call an "epidemic" of loneliness. Over half a century after the embrace of the sexual revolution—irrefutably, because of the embrace of the revolution—the paradox emerges that the materially better-off countries of the planet are also the most emotionally impoverished for many citizens, particularly though not only the elderly.

Toward the end of 2016, the *New York Times* published a harrowing story about what the birth dearth looks like from the other end of time's telescope: "'4,000 lonely deaths a week.'. . . Each year, some of [Japan's elderly] died without anyone knowing, only to be discovered after their neighbors caught the smell."[15] The story goes on to note that generations of empty cradles have also given rise to a new industry: firms that clean out the apartments of the isolated dead, because no family members remain to do it. According to another recent report in the *Independent*, such cleanup outfits are burgeoning, and insurance companies now offer policies to protect landlords in case a "lonely" happens on their property.[16]

And Japan is just one country facing the postpill demographic change that is rendering great numbers of elderly people into social isolates. *Le Figaro* reported several years ago that loneliness is a growing phenomenon in France.[17] Citing a study on the "new solitudes" by the Fondation de France, the article names the prime driver of this loneliness: "family rupture," especially divorce.

In similar vein, a 2014 study, "Socio-Demographic Predictors of Loneliness Across the Adult Life Span in Portugal," found that divorce increases the likelihood of loneliness—though it did not ask whether having children might ameliorate the problem.[18] Oddly, one can read through many loneliness studies without seeing reference to evolution's own implied cure for the vulnerability of creatures in old age (i.e., offspring).

In Sweden, a 2015 documentary on *The Swedish Theory of Love* told harrowing tales of lonely Scandinavian deaths. In Germany, *Der Spiegel* published an article titled "Alone by the Millions: Isolation Crisis Threatens German Seniors." There, the German Center of Gerontology reported that "one in four [Germans over 70] receives a visit less than once a month from friends and acquaintances, and nearly one in 10 is not visited by anyone anymore."[19]

It is imperative to absorb this grim spectacle and its testimony to the long-term effects of the unnaturally detached ways in which more and more of Western humanity now lives. Just as social science half a century ago was beginning to capture the effects of familial disruption on the young, so is sociology today mapping its effects on the old. The catastrophe of solitude among many of society's most vulnerable members is only beginning.

This loneliness is a new form of human poverty. It is abounding in societies awash in material wealth—places where, by the 1970s, divorce rates were going up, marriage rates were going down, and fewer bassinets were needed. It does not take a demographer to connect the dots between the social victory of recreational sex and the loneliness of the aged today. As one elderly German poignantly summarized in the aforementioned article in *Der Spiegel*: "Her husband didn't want any children. 'I should have insisted on it,' says the former cook, 'and then I perhaps wouldn't be so lonely today.'"

The arithmetic behind the new isolation is simple. Not only have divorce and cohabitation loosened the gravitational pull of family; simultaneously, contraception and abortion have also shrunk the nucleus further. The result is a new generation of elderly, some of whom reach the end of their years not only sans teeth and sight, but sans spouse, sans children and grandchildren.

This overlooked context explains the salience of another hot-button political issue, which is the press for easier access to euthanasia across the advanced nations. It does make social albeit sepulchral sense. Six decades into the changes catalogued by Robert D. Putnam, James Q. Wilson, and other social cartographers of the world we now know, substantial numbers of older people now hail from small, broken, isolated, and distant families. This means that many cannot count on offspring or other relatives to take them in for old age—in part because so many have left, or been left by, family members in the first place.

Loneliness is not the only vulnerability many Western seniors share. There is also the increased risk of physical harm.

Recall, for example, the disastrous heat wave of August 2003 that claimed some thirty-five thousand lives across Europe, with fourteen thousand of those in France. Most of those deaths were among the elderly. So disproportionately affected were they that a professor at the University of Wisconsin-Madison, Richard C. Keller, wrote a book titled *Fatal Isolation: The Devastating Paris Heat Wave of 2003*.[20]

This was in one sense a natural catastrophe, brought on by heat. But it was in another sense an unnatural catastrophe—one visited on thirty-five thousand people in some of the most advanced societies on earth. Though materially well off when measured by almost any standard of history, they were impoverished in another way: they were poor in family. Many died because they did not have what other human beings throughout history have been able to count on: loved ones to spirit them away from a disaster.

As the head of a major French funeral company put it, analyzing the data in retrospect, "many elderly people were left behind by vacationing families." (He added that some people, "informed of the death of relatives, postponed funerals—so as not to interrupt the Aug. 15 holiday weekend—and left the bodies in the refrigerated hall."[21])

Loneliness is no mere adolescent affectation. Social isolation on the scale found throughout the countries of the West is now exacting serious health costs that can be expected to rise as the Baby Boom generation enters its final years. Yet while senior citizens are the most visible objects of concern, including for companies that provide health services, they are not the only people so affected. One national survey conducted by Cigna whose results were released in May 2018 found that nearly half of all Americans report "sometimes or always" feeling alone, and that Generation Z—born between 1995 and 2010—is the loneliest generation of all.[22]

Big Health takes an interest in social atomization for sound reasons. In their 2008 book *Loneliness: Human Nature and the Need for Social Connection*, scientists John T. Cacioppo and William Patrick summarized a great deal of evidence linking atomization to health risks, including a literature review in *Science* indicating that social isolation is a risk factor for illness and death whose effects are comparable to other, more familiar ones: high blood pressure, obesity, lack of exercise, and smoking.[23] Cacioppo and Patrick also identified five "causal pathways" by which loneliness might be expected to undermine health—including overeating, higher stress hormones, cardiovascular conditions, and immune dysfunction.[24]

GONE GOD

There is another conventional way of knowing who we are that has also been mightily diminished during the past several decades: religious affiliation.

We live at a moment when more and more people have no experience of organized religion. As the Pew Research Center and other sources have been documenting for years, rising numbers of Americans, especially under the age of forty, are falling away from religious practice and religious literacy.

This trend has far-reaching implications for society, of course. The shrinking of the churches also reduces moral traditionalism, meaning that the same trends seen today can be expected to accelerate. In *How the West Really Lost God: A New Theory of Secularization*, I summarized what a variety of data has been indicating about the social consequences of religious decline. These include the effects of secularization on phenomena far from the churchyard itself, among them criminality, charitable giving, the size of the welfare state, health and longevity, aesthetic and historical literacy, and other unintended fallout of the receding Western God.[25]

At the same time, the diminution of active Christianity, in particular, has other consequences that no one has even begun to map. Secularization also means that many people no longer experience the opposite sex as those with a religious background are instructed to do—as figurative sisters and brothers, united in fellowship. Once more, people have been deprived of a familial, nonsexual knowledge of the opposite sex, and another healthy bond between the sexes has been frayed.

At its most fundamental, the vote by much of Western humanity to live without a transcendental horizon removes one more way of answering the question *Who am I?* that religion has traditionally supplied: *I am a child of God.*

If church, community, and family have all weakened markedly during the past half century, as measures indicate overwhelmingly, might any substitute institutions have emerged to take their places?

Certainly the expansion of the hours that children and teenagers spend in school would seem to qualify. The pressure to spend even more can be seen in changes like all-day kindergarten, before and after school care, and other measures of increased institutionalization. Perennial calls to expand the school day and to abolish summer vacation are driven by two factors: the extended amount of time that students in other nations spend in school and, above all, parental desire.[26] Surely, some would argue, these extra hours among peers amount to *some* kind of "socialization" for the great majority of Western young.

But the idea that educational institutions can substitute adequately for the lost languages of community and family elides several problems with this regimen that have become endemic: bullying;[27] violence;[28] and an apparent increase in child and adolescent psychiatric problems that parallels the rise seen in college students.[29] As with other social ills, the Internet amplifies all of these negatives, as researchers are now documenting in detail.[30]

Yet here as elsewhere, influential though they may be, the Internet and social media remain secondary to the essential problem. Schools now serve for many as substitute, substandard families. Whether government-run or otherwise, even the best schools amount to "forced packs," and exactly like the forced packs of nonhuman animals, they will produce winners and losers depending on the adaptive strategies of their institutionalized members. Students who succeed in dominating, or adapting to the new dominance schema, fare best. Others are left vulnerable to the heightened stresses of the artificial pack in ways that would not have existed in the natural, albeit receding, pack of their own.

Putting together these various large pieces, we glimpse a phenomenon that has come to characterize more and more lives during the past half century: what might be called "phantom" family members. Many postrevolutionary people, whether through choice or accident, now pass through life vaguely aware of lives that could have been, but weren't—whether because of domestic disruption in childhood, or the long string of exes now typical in Western mating, or abortion, or childlessness by choice, or other sources of what could be called family, interrupted.

Many of us live in patterns of serial monogamy, for instance, in which one partner is followed by another. When children are present, this means a consistently shifting set of family members to whom one is sometimes biologically related and sometimes not: stepfathers, half siblings, full siblings, nominal "uncles" and "cousins," and other permutations that mimic and serve to substitute for the family of one's biological relations.

As couples form and unform, as people find new partners and shed old ones, these relations morph with them. The result for many people is the addition and subtraction of "family" members on a scale that was unimaginable until reliable contraception for women, followed by the related legalizing of abortion, made the deinstitutionalization of traditional marriage and family possible.

A famous children's book by P. D. Eastman published in 1960 bears the title—teasing, under the circumstances—*Are You My Mother?* In it, a baby bird goes from one creature to another trying to find one like him, finally to be united in a happy maternal ending. To get an inkling of how the world has been transformed, imagine playing something like that game today.

Is that your stepsister? Maybe yes—*if* your mother is still married to that person's biological father. If instead this parental unit has split up, though, and her father has moved with his daughter to a new state, and acquired a new stepmother and new stepsiblings, likely no.

Is that your uncle? This too depends entirely on what other adults in the picture have decided to do. If your so-called uncle was your mother's boyfriend several boyfriends ago, and she hasn't seen him in years, then you and he are probably not "related" anymore—or anyway, would be unlikely to describe yourselves as such.

On the other hand, if that "uncle" is your biological father's biological brother, then likely the bond still holds—even if your biological mother and father never married.

Is that your niece? If she's your sister's biological or adopted child, you'd probably say yes. But if instead she's your sister's new live-in boyfriend's child from a previous liaison of his, you'd probably hesitate. By similar logic, the adult children of a man who takes a wife their age are unlikely to refer to her as "Mom."

And round and round the game of musical identity chairs goes. The result of all these shifting and twirling selves is that many people no longer know what humanity once knew across history: a reliable circle of faces, many of them biologically related to oneself, more or less consistently present during early and adolescent life and also thereafter.

For all kinds of reasons and for all kinds of people, those faces are receding. Wherever any one of us stands in matters of the "culture wars" is immaterial here. The plain fact is that the relative stability of yesterday's familial identity could not help but answer the question at the heart of identity politics—*Who am I?*—in ways that many men, women, and children can't answer it any more.

In sum, the diminution and rupture of the human family and the rise of identity politics are not only happening at the same time. They cannot be understood apart from one another. Anthropological evidence from every culture and era verifies that human beings by their nature live in families—just as coyotes and elephants and many other mammals live in families, rather than in random collections of individuals of the same species. Evidence also shows that human beings across history have gravitated toward religious communities of some kind. Broadly speaking, and *pace* the outlier that is the postrevolutionary West, both family and faith have been integral, unbidden demands of our kind just about everywhere else human beings have been found. They have been the default ways of answering the question *Who am I?*

And now many who are less acquainted with either can no longer figure out how to supply those demands—or perhaps even to understand them as perennial needs of our species in the first place.

3

Supporting Evidence, I

UNDERSTANDING THE "MINE!" IN IDENTITY POLITICS

Thus far, we have seen that the sexual revolution has frayed as never before the familial bonds of the social creature we know best. Returning to the point about the multiplicity of causes behind any large social phenomenon, it bears repeating here that the revolution is not the only force weakening those connections.

To name a few others, the geographic and class mobility of the United States have long enabled self-invention and reinvention on a scale hitherto unknown—which is why F. Scott Fitzgerald's famous line in *The Last Tycoon* about "no second acts in American lives" is one with which the author himself likely disagreed.[1] Air travel, satellites, and other cogs of globalization have also uprooted families and communities. Another factor is the technology of mass communication. In *Bowling Alone*, Robert D. Putnam made the case that television, in particular, has had a substantial negative effect on social participation.[2] And as seen over and over, there is the Janus-faced Internet, simultaneously connecting and dividing as never before.

Nonetheless, to acknowledge that other seismic shifts have also weakened the foundations of identity is not to minimize the overwhelming evidence presented in the preceding chapter—all of it pointing to something genuinely new under the sun. More people are living with looser ties to kith and kin than ever before; this change is systemic, and it cannot help but make the question *Who am I?* harder to answer than it used to be.

As G. W. F. Hegel described, and as political scientist Francis Fukuyama discussed in his 2018 book *Identity: The Demand for Dignity and the Politics of Resentment*, the desire for recognition is a powerful, often unseen mover in human affairs.[3] So what happens in a world where *ordinary* means of achieving recognition—within a family as a father, uncle, cousin, brother, mother, grandfather, and so forth—have been reduced by the Great Scattering?

One thing that seems to happen is some people, deprived of recognition in the traditional ways, will regress to a state in which their demand for recognition becomes ever more insistent and childlike. This brings us to one of the most revealing features of identity politics: its infantilized expression and vernacular.

Consider, for starters, a phenomenon especially baffling to people who are not part of identity politics: the widespread and seemingly inexplicable frenzy over "cultural appropriation." According to Oxford Dictionaries, this is "the unacknowledged or inappropriate adoption of the customs, practices, ideas, etc. of one people or society by members of another and typically more dominant people or society."[4]

One emblematic eruption over "appropriation" occurred at Yale University in 2015, when the university's Intercultural Affairs Committee preemptively asked students in advance of Halloween to avoid certain costumes that might offend. In response, faculty member Erika Christakis offered a mild demurral, suggesting in an email the logical consequences of such a policy (e.g., that it might bar blonde toddlers, say, from dressing up as Asian characters in a Disney film).[5] Her dissent sparked a protest letter signed by hundreds of students, an ugly public confrontation between menacing students and Christakis's husband, a social media campaign against them both, and headline news.

And Yale's costume controversy has been only the most visible example of the weaponization of dress-up. In 2015, the president of the University of Louisville issued a public apology after it was revealed that he and a group of friends had worn sombreros and other Mexican-themed attire. Surveying costume parameters handed down lately by authorities at Tufts University, one writer summarized how far restrictions now extend, noting that "students who heed the above guidelines are presumably restricted from dressing up as samurais, hombres, geishas, belly dancers, Vikings, ninjas, rajas, French maids, Bollywood dancers, Rastafarians, Pocahontas, Aladdin, Zorro, or Thor."[6]

Even lingerie peddlers aren't immune from the politics of appropriation. In one 2016 show, Victoria's Secret was outed in the fashion pages not because of what its models weren't wearing, ironically, but because of what they were: accessories that made sartorial reference to Chinese New Year, Native American headdresses, and other wearable cultural symbols, now seen in the appropriation age as taboos.[7]

Again, to perplexed bystanders who think a bongo drum is just a bongo drum and that tacos can be enjoyed by everyone, the cacophony over cultural "ownership" makes no sense. That's why those who protest along these lines are written off as "snowflakes," say, or as the supposed products of "helicopter parenting" (i.e., spoiled brats).

But what if the truth lies somewhere else—in a different direction from "coddling" theories?

"Mine! Mine! It's mine!"

What critics of identity politics have missed is that the manifest panic behind cries of cultural appropriation is real—as real as the tantrum of a toddler. It's as real as the developmental regression seen in the retreat to "safe spaces" on campus, those tiny ersatz treehouses stuffed with candy, coloring books, and Care Bears. It's as suggestive as the pacifiers that were all the rage as campus accoutrement in the 1990s.[8]

In social science, the toddler's developmental "Mine!" is known as the "endowment effect"—the idea that human beings ascribe extra value to possessions in virtue of the fact that they are theirs. Some scholars also see in the endowment effect a variation of another human proclivity: loss aversion.[9]

The evidence is impressionistic. But maybe that cultural scream of "Mine!" is coming from people who *did* have something taken from them, whether individually or collectively—only something more substratal than the totemic objects now functioning as figurative blankies for lost and angry former children. Maybe the furor over appropriation unveils the true foundation of identity politics, which is pathos.

The outsize agitations over what's "Mine!" are also uncannily suggestive of sibling rivalry, in which a younger one struggles with an older, "dominant" sibling for possession of a toy. The court of public opinion in which these increasingly frenzied controversies now play out is, in effect, the figurative parent to whom the weaker sibling appeals for equity.

It is not only the language of cultural appropriation that conjures the familial point. The regression to a childlike state can be found all over the dialects of identity politics.

This includes those of the alt-right and racialist European-firsters. "Mine!" is the primal cry, for example, of the white nationalists yearning for an "ethnostate." One such group—the American Identity Movement, formerly Identity Evropa—defined "decolonization" as "a giant civilizational game of 'what is mine is mine, and what is yours is also mine'"—a phrase literally ripped from a popular T-Shirt for toddlers.[10] Incidentally, one pathbreaking 2018 study of white nationalists by the Institute for Family Studies at the University of Virginia turned up another finding that is grist for the mill of this book's thesis of a link between domestic dispossession and identitarianism: white nationalists are much more likely to be divorced than married or never married.[11]

In a 2017 analysis of the writings of the alt-right called *Kill All Normies: Online Culture Wars From 4Chan And Tumblr to Trump and the Alt-Right*, Angela Nagle speculated that "the central personal motivation behind the entire turn to the far right among young men" can be found in the poor prospects they now face for finding happiness in building a family:

> The sexual revolution that started the decline of lifelong marriage has produced great freedom from the shackles of loveless marriage and selfless duty to the family for both men and women. But this ever-extended adolescence has also brought with it the rise of adult childlessness and a steep sexual hierarchy. Sexual patterns that have emerged as a result of the decline of monogamy have seen a greater level of sexual choice for an elite of men and a growing celibacy among a large male population at the bottom of the pecking order.[12]

This mention of involuntarily celibate men—so-called "incels"—brings us to one more aggrieved identity group created by the postpill sexual disorder, and nothing else. The incel movement came to national attention in 2018, when a man who identified himself as such killed ten pedestrians in the worst act of terror committed with a vehicle in Toronto's history.[13] As with other identity groups, there is more than one cause feeding the phenomenon of incel-ism. The group's characteristic misogyny, for example, is likely exacerbated by similar themes in the pornography to which incels often refer.[14] And, as seen before, no doubt finding one another on the Internet further inflames the senses of loss, rage, and belligerence.

At the same time, though, and as is also true of other identitarian subsets, social media per se did not create this furious collection of the purportedly deprived. The first cause behind this identity group can only be the post-1960s sexual chaos—with its unbridgeable chasm between the prelapsarian promise of pleasure for all and the gritty reality of nonnegotiable, new social hierarchies formed to adapt to the new ecosystem. The incel phenomenon is the face of Tantalus in our time.

To point out the similarities in emotional expression among identity-firsters isn't to posit moral equivalence between neo-Nazis and Black Lives Matter. It is also not to overlook the genuine grievances, sufferings, and injustices visited on individual members. Indeed, this book would not exist without the conviction that beneath the noise of identity politics lie authentic hardships, including antediluvian ones that have not been hitherto acknowledged.

Returning to the example of Victoria's Secret, it makes sense that Native Americans would find offensive the spectacle of a mostly-naked woman of European descent, parading in headgear of great cultural and religious significance. It also makes sense that African Americans—and others—object to the enshrining of past public figures known for their racism. The point here is not the objections, which a more reasonable society could discuss case-by-case. It is rather the preternaturally emotive language in which identitarian claims are typically expressed.

Something has been taken from me and my people, a wrong that my leaders must right: that is the unspoken shared refrain. In the same way, the term "woke" of the progressive left and the term "red pill" of the alt-right are words from different glossaries, describing the same epiphany: the moment at which one found the *figurative* family/community to do what *literal* families/communities of earlier times did by default (i.e., have your back, surround you with like-minded sympathizers, and explain the world and your place in it).

For another example of infantilism in identity politics, recall the mentions earlier of the bizarre behavior of protestors at various controversial public talks—the crying, the chanting and stomping, the seeming inability in case after case to respond to authority and reason. One more instantiation was an outburst that greeted Jordan B. Peterson at McMaster University in 2017.[15] Like other speakers subjected to such abuse, he commented afterward on the wrongs done to the cause of free speech by people with a bullhorn chanting the same repetitive interruptions. Once again, though, free speech was not the only public good being imperiled. Video of the event captures scores of people screaming and chanting nonstop, almost entirely in monosyllables—a spectacle less reminiscent of a civil rights protest than of, say, the menacing one-word chants of the frenzied in chapter 9 of *Lord of the Flies*.

In sum, the chronic regression to preadolescent language and behavior is testimony to something important about identity politics: its prerational origins.

In October 2018, following the confirmation of Supreme Court Justice Brett Kavanaugh, a Democratic political consultant delivered a raw and widely read exercise in identitarianism called "White Women, Come Get Your People."[16] Most remarkable was its final image, in which the author described being unable to hear talk of "due process and some other nonsense" due to her "rage headache." Such is the very incarnation of a toddler tantrum, complete with fingers in ears, ignoring adult conversation.

Identity politics is *pre*politics. But is not only a pediatric tantrum. To those who can no longer find their selves through the usual means, it is also a survival strategy for a postrevolutionary world, as the next two chapters explain.

4

Supporting Evidence, II

FEMINISM AS SURVIVAL STRATEGY

To say that identity politics amounts to a survival strategy is not to impute conscious strategic action to identitarians—any more than the Amur leopard has to think about the rosettes on his coat that will help him blend into the broadleaf forest. Strategies do not have to be conscious; they only have to *work*. I will test that proposition in this chapter by way of understanding the adaptive benefits of one particularly long-running form of identity politics, the one dating back to the founding document of the Combahee River Collective: contemporary feminism.

Feminism has come a long way since the 1960s. It seems safe to say that yesterday's Suffragettes would find what happens in the name of women's rights today unrecognizable. To the political left, for example, the Women's March on Washington, DC, following the election of Donald Trump was a heartwarming affirmation of "resistance." Others watched the same footage and saw something different: anger, belligerence, and obscenity.

Indeed, where one stood on the Women's March was more or less a litmus test for red and blue America.[1]

The atmospherics of the march revealed a marked transformation in the movement known as feminism. Over fifty years ago, Susan Sontag wrote of what she called "camp sensibility," a label that signaled an ethos defined by artifice, stylization, "neutrality concerning content," and overall "apoliticism."[2] Today's feminism exhibits a far more emotive and wrenching sensibility. Its language is purposefully tough and vulgar, a filtering of reality that is deliberately stripped of decoration or nicety, and instantaneous at taking offense.

Consider popular music by several artists who invoke the feminist label. In the song "Slut Like You," a quintessential anthem, self-described feminist singer Pink mocks the idea of falling in love, via liberal use of the s-word and related raunch. A 2010 video by singer Ciara, costarring a mechanical bull, was so problematic that Black Entertainment Television (BET) declined to air it. Many feminist singers also throw a pole dance or an homage to leather into their videos. Kesha, Britney Spears, the defunct Pussycat Dolls, Madonna: the trick isn't finding a female vocal artist and self-described feminist whose work is enthusiastically pornographic—it's locating any whose is not.

Feminists and progressives, of course, embrace this kind of rough-and-tough pose; moral traditionalists and others outside the woke population are baffled by it. My point is different: such coarseness is a *strategy*. Some might say it was ever thus—that feminism has always been angry. But there is a difference between the peevishness behind, say, "A woman needs a man like a fish needs a bicycle," and the purposely lewd and crude language characteristic of feminism today. Think again of the emblematic hats at the Women's March and what they made a household name. Measuring just by its profanity, today's feminism is not your mom's after all.

Obscenity is no mere pressure valve. It's a form of anger and aggression unto itself, spewed by people who feel threatened. Consider by way of example Miley Cyrus, former Disney child star turned feminist leader and identity poster person, explaining to *V Magazine* about her art: "Everything just kept sh**ting on me and sh**ting on me. So then I started taking all of those sh** things and making them good, and being like, I'm using it. . . . So, that's how I started making art. I had a bunch of f***ing junk and sh**, and so instead of letting it be junk and sh**, I turned it into something that made me happy."[3]

Verbal aggression is often directed within feminist ranks at other feminists. Feminist bell hooks, for instance, slammed singer Beyoncé as a "terrorist" for "her impact on young girls."[4] One feminist said of another, Tina Fey, that her "'nerdy' onscreen persona and adamant faux feminism masks a Thatcherite morality and tendency to slut-shame."[5] Typical feminist blogs and magazines likewise go after their own, like entries in "Mean Girls Gone Wild." In 2015, commenting on the ubiquity of "slut," "slut-shaming," "slutty," "slut walks," and related parlance now common within feminist discourse, the *New York Times* produced a dominatrix who identified as a "feminist/intellectual/queer" to report that "it pains and frustrates me to see this kind of judging and conflict within feminist communities."[6]

What everyone outside this rough and otherwise opaque conversation needs to understand is something that both right and left have so far missed. However unconsciously, feminism is in fact expressing an overlooked truth here: today's women have reason to feel cornered.

After all, violence and implied violence are all over popular culture—as exhibited by the phenomena of *Fifty Shades of Grey*, by music videos "exploring" sadomasochism, and above all, by pornography, in which the infliction of pain is a common add-on.[7] These and other cultural signs point toward a truly frightening appetite out there, sated only by watching women get hurt.[8] Sexual harassment in the workplace and elsewhere has apparently become commonplace, as women with #MeToo stories are the first to claim. Wherever they are on the political spectrum, many Western women do not experience the sexual revolution and its empowering of male predation as a golden age.

All of which leads, finally, to a sad and monumental fact that has been understood neither by a left that embraces feminist identities nor by a right that dismisses them. Feminism has become something very different from what it understands itself to be, and indeed from what its adversaries understand it to be. It is not a juggernaut of defiant liberationists successfully playing offense. It is instead an ultimately self-defeating but profoundly felt protective reaction to an environment of heightened risks. In a world where laissez-faire sex has made male companionship more peripatetic than before, some women will take on the protective coloration of male characteristics—blustering, cursing, belligerence, defiance, and also, as needed, promiscuity, or at least shout-outs thereto.

These signature attributes of today's "feminism" do not exist in a vacuum. However unconscious, they are strategies designed to compensate for the postrevolutionary strengthening of predatory men, the paucity of enduring positive male attention—and the paucity of male protection.

Again, the arithmetic is simple. The sexual revolution reduced the number of men who could be counted on to serve as protectors from time to time, and in several ways. Broken homes put father figures at arm's length, at times severing that parental bond for good. The ethos of recreational sex blurred the line between protector and predator, making it harder for many women to tell the difference. Simultaneously, the decline of the family has reduced the number of men offering affection and companionship of a nonsexual nature—fewer brothers, cousins, uncles, and others who could once have been counted on to push back, figuratively or otherwise, against other men treating mothers or sisters or daughters badly. Also simultaneously, the overabundance of available sexual partners has made it harder to hold the attention of any one of them—as has the diminished social and moral cachet of what was once the ultimate male attention-getter, marriage.

The result is that many women have been left vulnerable and frustrated. The furious, swaggering, foul-mouthed rhetoric of feminism promises women what many can't find elsewhere: *protection*. It promises to constrain men in a world that no longer constrains them in traditional ways. Into this vacuum of vulnerability, feminism speaks an implied message of ostensible hope: *we will rein men in by other means.*

This is the deeper unrecognized allure of draconian speech codes on campuses and elsewhere: they promise to limit what men can do and say, in a world in which the old limits on male behavior no longer apply. Once again, to say that such a strategy is operating outside of conscious agency is not to deny its objective reality; animals, including human animals, respond unconsciously to social and other cues all the time, whether in the form of pheromones or subliminal advertising or other signals that register without our realizing it.

The question is whether feminism as postrevolution survival strategy will succeed in the long run—about which there is ample room for doubt. As noted, women, for all their empowerment on other fronts, are also now more vulnerable than before, thanks to the changes wrought by the very revolution that feminism embraces. This is the unspoken, unacknowledged truth beneath today's acrimonious and ultimately tragic conversation.

Feminism is a case study linking identity politics with the blasted familial landscape. Many women are now exactly what feminist identitarians say they are: victims—only not in the way

5

Supporting Evidence, III

ANDROGYNY AS SURVIVAL STRATEGY

Just as a bellicose feminism offers protection of sorts in the postrevolutionary order, so might the blurring of lines in another area: sexual identity.

Many people—mainly, many older people who themselves grew up in a less cumulatively fractured time—have found the proliferating of "gender identities" to be the most baffling phenomenon of the day. Stories about gender have become nonstop in the news cycle and popular culture. It is impossible to know nothing of them, whether the focus is on celebrities like Caitlyn Jenner, or the changes being demanded of grammar regarding pronouns, or biological boys playing on girls' sports teams,[1] or hormonal and surgical "transitioning," or Facebook's seventy-one different gender options, or other manifestations of the drive to construct identities independent of all limitations, including chromosomal constraint.

And yet, I would argue, for all the attention lavished on questions of sex and gender, the trees have obscured the forest before us. The increased expression of ambiguous sexuality reflects a deeper metamorphosis that has been underway since the 1960s, of which today's obsession with gender identity is but a part. That is the gravitation toward an androgynous mean, forced by the sexual revolution's reconfiguring of the human ecosystem. It is a story that begins at the very dawn of the revolution, with its tell-tale unisex costume for all: blue jeans.

Coined by British journalist Mark Simpson in 1994, the term "metrosexual" is another manifestation of androgyny's spread. On a pointillist note, "man buns" and the rapidly expanding market niche of male makeup would seem to qualify too.[2] Like the other varied cultural phenomena considered in this book as manifestations of postrevolutionary change, this one extends beyond the United States. An increase in androgynous expression is now to be found around the world—specifically, in societies transformed by the postrevolutionary remaking of primordial ties. Contrary to what some tradition-minded critics have suggested, the politics of sexual identity is no boutique passing fad of blue America. It is a global expression of more subterranean forces.

Why? Like feminism, androgyny appears to offer competitive advantages in a world ruled by the Great Scattering. It is a way of augmenting one's substitute clan. It operates, in effect, as a mechanism for reconstructing the extended family/community in prosthetic form in a time when the actual Western extended family/community is in decline.

As therapists and their clients and a growing body of literature affirm, gender dysphoria comes with crippling psychological distress.[3] It is no disservice to its victims to observe that there might be wider environmental changes that have increased the attraction of gender fluidity and ambiguity. Like feminism, the new virtual gender communities offer what in-person communities used to: connections, an audience, a sympathetic ear, and a relational answer to the question *Who am I?*

The question of sexual *behavior* is extraneous here. Identitarians often say that gender identity is about more than sex. Let us take their point empathetically and examine what other forces might be operating in that "more" space.

To get a sense of how pervasive androgyny has become throughout Western culture, consider a few facts.

For many years now, sex differences in strength and endurance have been ignored or minimized and standards for physical fitness altered, in the armed forces, police and fire departments, and other venues where physical strength matters.[4] As one consequence among many, for the first time in American history, young American women stand a chance of being drafted into combat positions.[5]

From the most serious manifestations to the seemingly trivial, increased if inchoate demands for androgyny have proliferated. Even retail stores have been reconfigured by this amorphous force. Under pressure from gender activists, to name one among hundreds of examples, a major retail chain agreed to eliminate all "gender-based signage" in its toy, home, and entertainment sections and clarified that in the toy section, it would even cease using "pink, blue, yellow, or green paper on the back walls of our shelves." So reported Ashley McGuire in *Sex Scandal: The Drive to Abolish Male and Female* (2017)—the first book-length treatment of its subtitle, and the best compendium so far of the many realms in which the new androgyny is rewriting the "binary."[6]

There is also the explosion of gender ambiguity and fluidity in popular culture, beginning, though not only, in the United States. MTV, following the new ideological regimen, in 2017 moved to "gender-neutral" awards for acting (i.e., no more separate awards for "actors" and "actresses"). Other vetting boards in the performing arts and related circles are following suit. Or consider another territory where androgyny has been reigning with little comment for a longer time: fashion.

Denim jeans, as mentioned, became the first sartorial plumage signifying the interchangeability of the sexes. In the 1990s, a handful of designers like Helmut Lang, Giorgio Armani, and Pierre Cardin pioneered what was called "unisex" clothing. Today, it is hard to name a major designer who hasn't reinforced the trend and gone further.

In Japan, designers like Comme des Garcons, Yohji Yamamoto, and Kenzo Takada render Asian versions of the same androgynous cool seen in Europe.[7] At Tokyo Fashion Week in spring 2017, one show featured eight male and four female models, all sporting intersex sartoria. Japanese fashion sources report that "genderless kei [style]" has been the hottest trend since 2015—when androgynous boys appeared at the Tokyo Girls fashion show, after which the look took off.[8] These are "generally slim-bodied and cute-faced boys who dye their hair, wear makeup and colored contact lenses, nail polish, flashy clothing, and cute accessories . . . rejecting traditional gender rules to create a new genderless standard of beauty."[9]

India is another country where cutting-edge fashion is embracing the unisex look. As one young designer put it: "For me, it is more an expression of power rather than gender. Power has traditionally been associated with men. Through androgynous silhouettes, there is a sense of power being transferred to women. Making women look more masculine than men—not only does this change gender stereotypes, but it is also an empowering gesture."[10]

As another essay on Indian fashion noted, it is easier to put women in male-style suits than it is to garb men in dresses.[11] This finding, too, is consonant with the analysis of the preceding chapter: women gravitate toward male gear more readily because it amounts to protective coloration; women remain the weaker players in the new ecosystem.

The impulse to propel male and female toward an androgynous middle is especially suggestive in the cases of India and China. In both countries, a combination of gross state coercion (China's "one-child" policy) and longstanding son preference have produced unprecedented demographic deformity: by some accounts, there are now over 50 million "excess" males in the two countries, and many of these prized sons will never marry or have children—in cultures where marrying and having children are held to make a man, a man.[12] If that is not grounds for identity confusion en masse, by the way, what is?

Androgyny is also front and center in popular music—and has been, for a while now. Once, David Bowie was a lone, mildly sexually ambiguous figure on the rock scene. Today, stars who flirt with gender bending are assured not only of fan love, but also of a field that gets more crowded by the day.

To repeat, androgyny's rewriting of popular culture isn't an expression of European or American sexual exceptionalism. As with fashion, the pop music trend is just as pronounced on the other side of the planet. Androgyny is a staple of Korean and Japanese popular genres, from K-pop and J-pop to anime and manga. Japan is also home to the phenomenon of "herbivores," meaning men who "live gently," including by avoiding sex—lately the subject of worried commentary in a country already over a demographic precipice.[13]

The hottest recent "boy band" in China is actually a collection of several androgynous girls.[14] Jin Xing—called the "Oprah of China" for having the most popular television talk show—was not only born male but is a former colonel in the People's Liberation Army.[15] And on the catalogue goes. "Girls just wanna have fun," Cyndi Lauper sang in a pop anthem nearly forty years ago. Judging by the global music scene, "girls just wanna be boys" might be more like it. And vice versa.

Of course androgyny is not the only sexualized theme discernible in contemporary pop culture. Anime and manga, for instance, also skew toward extremes of hypermasculinity and hyperfemininity, as does the pornified female music mentioned earlier. Even so, in society after society, it is androgyny that is most visible across the genres of fashion, music, and other byways of pop culture. Surely it is interesting to wonder why.

Plainly, something unprecedented is happening to humanity across the world—something so hitherto unknown, and operating with such power, that it demands more than passing explanation. Here's one thesis: The new androgyny is not incidental to the collapse of family and community. To the contrary, the new androgyny is being driven by the collapse of family and community.

I am arguing here for a new interpretation of the scene, according to which transgender bathrooms and related controversies are manifestations of a bigger and more abiding story: the ways in which the Great Scattering has increased pressure to gravitate away from the traditionally masculine and feminine and instead toward a more ambiguous, androgynous mean.

Economists say that to subsidize something is to ensure more of it. And this is essentially what the sexual revolution has done: it has inadvertently subsidized androgyny by raising the penalties for traditional masculinity and femininity. Let us count some ways.

As we have already seen in the example of feminism, acting more "male" via coarsened language or belligerent demeanor amounts to protective coloration. If men cannot, or will not, be found to help protect women (and children), to whom does that task fall? The answer would seem to be, a woman—a woman who's being more like a man, that is.

Another way in which the revolution would appear to have increased the incentive for women to act like men is more occult: the shrinkage of the family has reduced the number of fathers who have sons. Statistically, men—with some interesting exceptions that I'll get to—desire sons.[16] This does not mean that daughters go unloved but to note an interesting fact. Postrevolutionary man, deprived of the likelihood of a son by contraception, abortion, and other practices, might logically if unconsciously respond by pressuring daughters to behave more like sons.

Such pressure might explain some of the impetus behind the well-known rise in girls' participation in the most combative of sports, including ice hockey, football, soccer, and other contact games.[17] None of this list is intended to dispute the beauty of female athletics, or the manifest good of physical fitness. It is to note instead that women and girls are more vulnerable to injury in contact sports than are men and boys, for several reasons including higher estrogen levels, a wider pelvis, narrower space within the anterior cruciate ligament (ACL), and a higher likelihood of inadequate calcium and vitamin D intake.[18] So what does it tell us that it is now socially acceptable for them to assume higher physical risks than they did before, with a commensurately higher likelihood of injury?

It tells us that society has "decided," again, that there is some kind of enhanced value to women behaving more like men.

Decided is in quotation marks for good reason: because the parents and coaches of the world nowhere sat down and took a vote, thereby agreeing as a matter of policy that the time had come to put women and girls at increased physical risk. To the contrary, authorities like parents and coaches have responded instead to social cues and collective pressure—meaning the radically altered incentive system in an ecosystem of smaller families, fewer communal ties, and the rest of the post-1960s record.

Anecdotal evidence confirms the trend. Consider the perennial commentary sprung from soccer fields, baseball fields, hockey rinks, and basketball courts across the country about the behavior of some parents—in particular, fathers yelling themselves hoarse at their girls for not being stronger or faster or more aggressive . . . for not being more like boys. As one conflicted mother, faced with just such a belligerent father at a girls' middle-school basketball game, put it: "I got involved and tried to remind this lovely father that we weren't drunk fans at a WWE event, but parents of 13- and 14-year-old young women, whom, I think, we are encouraging to play sports in an effort to increase their self-esteem, give them more confidence and empower them to stand up for themselves when necessary."[19]

Sports are only one of the more visible arenas where the renorming of women toward men has become routine. The bedrock fact is that today's women are continually given the message that they must perform like men—that *men* are the standard by which *women* should be measured. It is a pernicious comparison for several reasons, one of them described by Ashley McGuire when she observes that women who cannot, or do not, compete on male terms—sexually, athletically, professionally, or otherwise—are then trapped in the paradigm of being "failed men." A successful woman these days is most often one who behaves most like a man, in the workplace and elsewhere, and what might be called a "beta woman" is one who does not.

These are just some of the unforeseen outcomes of a cultural incentive system that has increased the rewards for women to behave in stereotypically male ways and reduced the social approbation for those who would persist in traditional female ways—marrying, raising a family of size, devoting time and talent to what used to be called domestic arts, volunteering, and otherwise contributing to the world apart from the paid marketplace.

In sum, from popular culture to sports, from schooling to the home, women who "lean in" toward the masculine are substantially more likely to be rewarded in the postrevolutionary order than women who do not. This fact alone amounts to a powerful engine driving the new androgyny.

And men?

For a different set of reasons, there is increased pressure in a postrevolutionary age *not* to act like men and to lean in toward the potentially more rewarding feminine side instead.

In 1999, biological anthropologist Lionel Tiger published a book called *The Decline of Males: The First Look at an Unexpected New World for Men and Women.*[20] He argued that contemporary feminism and legalized abortion rendered men less effective and less necessary than ever before. In a world where men have little legal or social say in the important matters of fatherhood and marriage, Tiger suggested, a great many might get the notion: why bother? The years since then seem to have vindicated his thesis in full, with "Peter Pan syndrome," video-gaming boys downstairs, "failure to launch," and other pop manifestations of the phenomenon he described. These forms of male retreat, too, have parallels elsewhere in the world, including in the *hikikomori* of Japan (boys who refuse to leave the basement and/or join society)[21] and the related "new hermits" of Korea.[22]

At the same time, these developments have illuminated another key point. Traditional masculinity is not only *unwanted* by many people in a postrevolutionary world where women now control (if they want to) the literal means of (re)production. Masculinity and men are also objects of new denigration, as the popular phrase "toxic masculinity," among other signposts, reveals.[23] The same stigmatization is also inadvertently responsible in part for the global embrace of Jordan B. Peterson's work by young men, especially; as psychologists would say, his affirmative writing gives them "permission" to be masculine at a time when masculinity is deemed déclassé and worse by nouveau tastemakers.[24]

The animosity toward masculinity doesn't spring from nowhere. Masculinity is in part *taught*—and as Tupac Shakur so plaintively pointed out, in an age when half of children don't have fathers, who will teach it? This brings us to another pressing (albeit resolutely unattended) phenomenon that increases the penalty for masculinity: the psychologically untenable situation in which many boys are caught, postrevolution.

As noted, some children today are born to unmarried women; and whether their parents ever married or not, many will not grow up with their biological father present in the home. That much is familiar sociology.

But these same homes are not only missing a male adult. They are also, often enough, homes in which the absent male parent is openly resented—in which the mother is regarded (understandably so) as a heroic figure for doing as one human what ought to be the work of two. Unavoidably, in many such families, the notion that men are unreliable is not an abstract feminist prejudice, but a fact of life.

What kind of message is received, however unconsciously, by the male children growing up in such homes? It is the lesson that *men are bad.*

How could those domestic atmospherics do anything *but* complicate a young man's effort to answer the question *Who am I?* Hillary Clinton and other self-described feminists are fond of invoking the slogan, "The future is feminine." The social reality is that this is no mere campaign message. Many boys must now adapt to a human habitat in which their very DNA is problematic from birth onward. What are they to conclude, *except* for the converse of Henry Higgins's lament in *My Fair Lady*—that it would be better for a man to be more like a woman?

One final bit of evidence for the claim that men enjoy less social value today appeared in 2016, via a "lifestyle article" in the *New York Times*. It unveiled what once would have been a surprising thought: that today's forward-looking, nontraditional fathers—including the author of the *Times* piece—would, if they had their druthers, pick daughters over sons.[25] "Some men, like me, *fear* becoming fathers to sons [emphasis added]," he explained, adding evidence from blogs and websites showing that he was not alone. In addition, he cited the data that well-off white parents who use preimplantation genetic diagnosis select for females 70 percent of the time and that adoptive parents prefer girls over boys by at least a third. In the case of same-sex couples, he reported, that preference is even stronger.

At a minimum, attitudes toward the male human animal are changing at an unforeseen clip, especially in circles that are all-in for sexual correctness. These changes are dictated in part by ever more furious women, reacting to ever more distant men, and in part by anxious men who are learning the social lesson that the feminine is to be feared. It defies logic to maintain that the ongoing impassioned flight to collective identities is independent of such major alterations in the atmosphere.

Just as feminism shows women adapting to the new environment by appearing more masculine, so is there new social advantage for men in becoming less so. Applied collectively, ironically enough, androgyny spells the end of the species. But applied individually, it seems to enhance social survivability, as it offers both men and women new crypsis for a new age—and with it, ways of answering *Who am I?* that are different and more conflicted than they used to be.

6

Supporting Evidence, IV

HOW #METOO REVEALS THE
BREAKDOWN OF SOCIAL LEARNING

As we have seen, evidence that the human ecosystem has suffered massive perturbation is both widespread and compelling. Yet the significance of that perturbation is not limited to the effects now seen in individuals. That is because the human animal is a social animal: one primed like all other social animals for *social* learning. By reducing and atomizing those others from whom the individual might learn, the postrevolutionary order repeatedly interrupts the transmission belt of learning itself (including religious learning, as argued in my book *How the West Really Lost God*).

This fracturing of the learning curve now manifests itself politically not only in the panic over identity, but in the related, radically unforeseen, and powerful case in point known as #MeToo. The global sensation of #MeToo is one more mirror revealing that accustomed social ways of learning have become truncated and distant, with results unique to our uniquely disconnected times.

How, after all, do human beings learn in the first place? On the philosophical plane, no one has answered this question as thoroughly as the French-born philosopher René Girard.[1] Beginning with his intensive study of some of the greatest novelists and dramatists, Girard went on to develop a theory of human behavior that would rival Sigmund Freud's in its completeness.

Central to this psychology is Girard's insight into the question of why individuals desire what they desire. Contrary to focusing as other thinkers have on the autonomous actions of an individual—such as the notion, say, of an always-rational *homo economicus*—this philosopher emphasized the social character of human behavior. In particular, he argued, we learn to want what we want by *watching what others want*. Desire is learned behavior, "mimetic." Desire makes us rivals, and rivalry leads to violence: from these building blocks Girard went on to construct an elaborate theory of scapegoating and sacrifice as the hidden mechanisms of human history.

For our purposes, it is Girard's insight into the mimetic character of humanity that demands focus. Interestingly enough, his insistence on the *relational* nature of human learning seems lately to have garnered de facto ratification in some cutting-edge studies of animal psychology and behavior. As one recent essay published in *BioScience* noted, the past two decades have seen an "explosion" of new research as the social nature of animal learning has been revealed as never before. The result has been acute attention to "food choice, tool use, patterns of movement, predator avoidance, mate choice, and courtship." All of these and other behaviors once thought to have been inborn turn out instead to be shaped by observation and imitation of others.[2] For that same reason, new academic attention is also zooming in on "formal models of when animals choose to copy behavior, and which other animals' behavior they copy"—formulations that read as though lifted whole from the pages of Girard.

So far you may be thinking: so what if human and nonhuman animals learn in part by imitating others? In fact, nothing could matter more. If we become who we are in part by imitating others, then it matters a great deal from whom we are learning, whom we have access to, and which sources of potential social information may now be off-limits or harder to reach.

The phenomenon of #MeToo exhibits the truth behind every one of these dicta. It is one more example of how changes in the postrevolutionary order are now saturating and transforming politics and society. #MeToo is a form of identity politics in which victimhood answers the question, *Who am I?*, and in which the breakdown of social learning is manifest in every society to have joined and been influenced by the movement.

To say this is not to ignore the depredations of those men who have been justly accused of wrongdoing, any more than real racism is minimized by pointing out that whiteness does not explain the whole of identity politics. Quite apart from critical questions of guilt and innocence, the #MeToo movement exhibits in full what happens when great swaths of humanity are more socially illiterate than our forebears were, because the pool of those from whom we learn earliest and most naturally has diminished.

To understand, first, that "social learning" is not an abstraction but a vital conduit to survival skills, consider the plight of the treed cat.

As some kitty owners and the occasional firefighter have come to know, not all cats can climb down from trees. They can, apparently, ascend easily enough, thanks to retractable claws that curve in a direction helpful for going up. But getting out of the tree is a different matter. Some can do it, and some, to their potential peril, cannot. Why?

Animal experts Karen Pryor and Temple Grandin are among those to have considered the problem, and they conclude that the answer is: a breakdown in social learning. At some point, mother cats teach kittens how to descend from a tree—just as they teach their young a great many other things that were once thought to be "innate" feline behavior, including how to hunt, bury their waste, deal with live prey, approach an unknown person or dog, and so forth.[3] Cats that get stuck in trees, the theory goes, are cats that were taken from their mothers before the lesson about getting out of trees could be taught. Grandin, who grew up on farms, appears to clinch the point by observing that while she had known house cats to suffer this lack of learning, she had never once seen a barn cat (i.e., a cat that had remained with its family, where it could learn the skill eventually from example) do the same.[4]

Examples abound to prove that a great deal of animal behavior is *learned* behavior. As science has lately shown, for instance, meerkats do not innately understand how to protect themselves from scorpion stings; rather, older meerkats show their young by way of example the exact sequence of pinches by which a scorpion can be rendered safe. Patagonian killer whales are not born knowing how to develop the risky skill of beaching themselves in order to obtain seals; they are taught by older members of the pod, including parents. Tigers, cheetahs, caracals, and other felids model the behavior by which attentive offspring learn to bring down prey.[5] This recitation should not suggest that social learning is limited to mammals. It is widespread throughout the animal order, including among ants, lizards, birds, and fish, all of whom become fully what they are by learning from others of their kind.[6]

Let's come back to the problem of the cat that has gone up the tree and can't get down. That feline may seem a modest example of a breakdown in social learning. But scientists interested in what happens when animals are truly atomized have devised more extreme ways of testing the rules.

These include the famous—and today, infamous—experiments performed in the 1950s by psychologist Harry Harlow on newborn rhesus monkeys. In their book *Loneliness*, cited earlier, John T. Cacioppo and William Patrick summarize the results of Harlow's research thus:

> [Monkeys] deprived of tactile comfort and also raised in isolation from other monkeys developed additional behavioral aberrations, often severe, from which they never recovered. . . . They were overly aggressive with their playmates, and later in life they remained unable to form normal attachments. They were, in fact, socially inept—a decision that extended down into their most basic biological behaviors.[7]

Harlow's experiments proved a pertinent truth: monkeys deprived of other monkeys could not "do" what other monkeys do. Monkey "nature"—and by extension, the "nature" of other animals—will not provide a sufficient blueprint to behavior in the absence of community. The rhesus females raised in isolation could not mother; they were abusive or incompetent.[8] Even monkeys raised in cages where they could see and smell other monkeys, but were deprived of touching them, developed "autistic-like syndrome."[9]

This brings us to the #MeToo movement, which inadvertently reveals where decades of smaller, less functional families and more dissipated communities have led: to a massive failure of many men and women to learn some of the most basic facts about themselves and the opposite sex. This failure is one consequence of a system in which the old ways of learning social behavior—within families, from opposite-sex relatives, in churches, in small social associations, and in other venues closer to home than the world of screens—have ceased for many people to function as they once did. In their place, other and less effective ways of learning have been exposed as poor substitutes.

Let us count the ways in which the treed cat and the #MeToo movement intersect.

First, let us look at some of what has been revealed by those accused in the scandals (i.e., the men).

One salient point to be made in retrospect went missing in the unfolding of the scandals from October 2017 onward. That is the question of what, exactly, made #MeToo possible in the first place. Men behaving badly, as many noted at the time, isn't exactly viral news. But *a great many men* taking for granted the sexual availability of women, in one profession after another: that is new. That is something that only the Pill and related technologies could have made possible. Only in a world where sex is allegedly free of consequence would anyone dare to proposition women on the spot, over and over, as appears to have happened repeatedly in these scandals.

But the triumph of recreation-first sex is also connected to the scandals in another, more subterranean way. Returning to a point made earlier on, the shrinkage of the family has deprived many men of sisters and daughters. It has deprived many women of brothers and sons. And, of course, divorce and cohabitation have also deprived boys and girls of biological parents, particularly fathers.

And what might be the net effect of all that deprivation? A

world in which the sexes know less about one another than they used to; in which many women no longer know men as companions and protectors, but only as predators; in which many men know women mainly through the narratives they absorb in watching pornography, which has become a default stand-in for social learning about women and sex.

Reading the grislier details of the scandals, some wondered aloud, What's wrong with these men? Don't they have mothers, sisters, and other women in their lives? How could they act this way, if that were the case? The answer is that after the Great Scattering, many men lack exactly such textured, long-running, socially informative, nonsexual experiences of the opposite sex— just as many women lack them too.

As important, we also live at a moment when more and more people have no experience of organized religion—an institution that for all its shortcomings has been the go-to guide for behavioral codes across history. This trend has many implications for society, of course, only some of which have been mapped.

As social scientist Arthur C. Brooks has shown, for example, rising secularization can be expected to be inimical to the poor, not least because religious believers give substantially more to charities than do nonbelievers.[10] Many scholarly inquiries into health have also associated religious belief positively with longevity.[11] One analysis of more than twelve hundred studies found that religion was "consistently associated with better health and predicted better health over time."[12] Another study in *Demography* of a nationally representative sample of U.S. adults, conducted over nine years, reported that the data translate into "a *seven-year* difference in life expectancy at age 20 between those who never attend [church services] and those who attend once a week [emphasis added]."[13]

In the context of #MeToo, secularization also means that many people no longer experience the opposite sex as Christians and other religious believers are instructed to do—as members of a transcendent family, helping each other like siblings.

Again, behold the irony here. The revolution has made sex itself more ubiquitous than ever before. But it has also estranged men and women as never before, both by shrinking the family and by increasing the mistrust between men and women thanks to widespread sexual consumerism.

That includes, to repeat, the consumption of pornography, whose distorted accounts of relations between the sexes are generating social, political, and legal consequences. To offer an indicator unthinkable thirty years ago, Internet pornography use is now a major factor cited in divorces. One study using data from the 2006–2014 General Social Survey found that when men start watching pornography during marriage, the odds of divorce double, and for women who start watching the same, they triple.[14]

In his 2017 book *Cheap Sex: The Transformation of Men, Marriage, and Monogamy*, sociologist Mark Regnerus used a variety of data sets, including a new one of fifteen thousand subjects, to argue in part that pornography consumption is having interesting effects on both politics and identity.[15] By way of example, its use predicts both political attitudes and church attendance: 54 percent of "very liberal" men aged 24–35 reported having viewed pornography in the past week, as opposed to 31 percent of "very conservative" men. Regnerus also argued that pornography is having a liberalizing effect on the populace.[16]

Pornography's implied blueprints not only make the rounds—they are believed, and they affect personal behavior. When one major media man fell from grace toward the beginning of #MeToo, he said that, "I always felt I was pursuing shared feelings."[17] Awful as his conduct allegedly was, those words ring with authenticity. It seems safe to bet that many modern men—especially those without religious attachments, and including those cited for reprehensible behavior by #MeTooers—believe similarly that women are always and everywhere available and interested (i.e., in the *Playboy* philosophy from Hugh Hefner's time to the present). Pornography reinforces that fantasy.

To observe that social learning about the opposite sex is being undermined by pornographic narratives is not to excuse crimes and misdemeanors among the accused (or for that matter, the possibility of false accusations among some accusers). But it is to grasp just a little of the mass confusion that surrounds us. To employ an image, think of sculptor Frederick Hart's magnificent work called *Ex Nihilo*, on the front of Washington National Cathedral. It shows beautiful human beings emerging from chaos, as God creates the world. Many seekers of romance today seem the opposite of what Hart envisioned. They are instead beautiful human beings not arising from chaos, but plummeting into it like Dante's Paolo and Francesca—endlessly circling, and never really touching.

This brings us to the other party demonstrating that #MeToo represents a significant failure of social learning among human animals: the women. About this group, too, there remains an unexplored storyline—one underlining, again, that ordinary ways of handing down social lessons about the opposite sex have been interrupted, with the result that some people are consequently failing to learn them.

The victims in these accounts are young women—typically sophisticated careerists and graduates of elite schools. It is not the daughters of red states, or their counterparts in other countries, who have pioneered and built #MeToo. It is instead the better educated, female upper echelon of the meritocratic and other elite classes, many of them leaning left, who found themselves on the receiving end of unwanted attentions, sexual harassment, and possible crimes.

And one can read only so many of their reports without wondering about the most basic question: why were so many in harm's way in the first place? No, this is not about blaming victims; courts of law—which are more reliable than the court of public opinion—are making it clear that there *are* victims. Consider by way of analogy the advice to avoid bad neighborhoods at night. If someone ignores that advice and is mugged, he is still a victim. At the time, the advice was sound. In the case of #MeToo, related common sense seems to have gone missing. Throughout the literature of #MeToo, there is a cluelessness about relations between the sexes that almost defies understanding.

Many women seem not to have been taught the most basic protective lessons—like not entering a boss's hotel room at night. In fact, so socially vulnerable are these victims that they did not even know to stand up for themselves—*until an international movement gave them permission to do so*. They engaged in mimetic victimhood.

And in that fact, too, evidence about animal nature illuminates just how far many of us have now strayed from an organic model of social learning. Psychologist Susan Minetka conducted an apropos experiment at Northwestern University that began with this fact: Monkeys in the wild are terrified of snakes; they scream, gesticulate wildly, tear their gaze away, and otherwise manifest fear when they see one. Monkeys born into captivity do none of these things when faced with a snake. That's because snake fearing in monkeys is not something all monkeys just "do" naturally. It is, rather, *learned* behavior—taught in the natural order of things (i.e., the wild). There, monkeys learn to behave like monkeys by watching other monkeys—in the matter of the snakes, for the good reason that snakes are potentially dangerous to monkeys.

Minetka thought to test this proposition by exposing her fear-free captive monkeys to monkeys raised in the wild exhibiting snake fear. The fascinating result was that the fear-free monkeys, observing their terrorized peers, within *minutes* became terrorized themselves. Not only was the transformation surprisingly rapid, but even more interesting, it stuck. Once the formerly placid monkeys "understood" thanks to their peers that they should fear snakes, they feared them to the same degree ever afterward—and that fear could not be undone. In this case, primal fear proved mimetic. And in one more fascinating coda, the monkeys could not be similarly induced to fear other images, like a flower. *Something* in the captive monkeys, it seems, was predisposed to fear the snake—but it took the example of the terrified monkeys to transform that predisposition into a living, permanent fear.

Social learning is taught by others of one's kind. Surely that fact explains why, when the first stories of #MeToo came pouring out, many more followed, and a cultural backdraft exploded across the Western world. Why hadn't these stories been told in the first place? Maybe because a critical mass of women hadn't learned from anywhere else—home, fathers, brothers, mothers, cousins, uncles, grandparents, and others with their best interests in mind—that predatory men are to be avoided when possible and called out if they transgress. Instead, the victims of #MeToo learned this by watching the revelations of other women. They learned mimetically as adults what they had not learned or been taught, for whatever reason of faulty social transmission belts, earlier on.

Plainly, legions of highly educated young women are being launched into society and the paid marketplace with little protective gear. It is surely not a random fact that many are also increasingly bereft of father protectors: men to whom they could have turned in a time of trouble; men who could potentially blunt the designs of harassers and abusers; or even just men—or women—who could have acted as reality checks by suggesting that some behaviors might be over the line and should be reported. Throughout the unfolding sex scandals, there was no mention of fathers, or brothers, or male cousins of these afflicted women—men in their familial corner fending off or seeking to right the wrongs done to them. There were a few mentions of boyfriends playing a protective role. Very few.

That, too, is remarkable. True enough, many women have been socialized ideologically to believe they need no protection at all. But as #MeToo ironically demonstrates, this is a risky bet. So long as women are far more likely to be raped, so long as they are overwhelmingly and on balance the physically weaker sex, and so long as they bear primary responsibility for the draining experience of childbirth and the greater load of child-rearing, as anyone with a modicum of sanity knows they do: for all these reasons, it will remain in their interests to ally with other, stronger, less physically constrained fellow humans—typically, men.

Popular culture and behavioral studies ratify what left-wing ideology denies. In the popular country song "Cleaning This Gun (Come On in Boy)," singer Rodney Atkins imagines a father doing just that as a young man arrives to take his daughter out. Throughout, what's implied is that the latent fact of superior force will shape the boy's behavior toward that daughter for the better—in much the same way that ecologists in South Africa's Pilanesberg Park found in 2000 that introducing several older bull elephants was all that it took to stop the younger male elephants already there from lethal rampaging against rhinoceroses.[18] Many human beings, it seems, now lack the parallel implied force that kept those rambunctious younger elephants in line.

In sum, #MeToo suggests that the world after the sexual revolution is one in which many women, thanks to family shrinkage and breakup, have fewer ties to men who are not potential predators; in which many men, thanks to the same forces, have little or no intimate but nonsexual knowledge of the opposite sex, and unsound sexual tutelage in the form of pornography; in which fundamental truths about disparities of size and strength are denied for ideological reasons; and in which the question of *romantic* identity for many is confounded by all of the above.

Whom do I love? is another way of answering *Who am I?* But in a world where many are not socialized to love as human animals have been socialized before, it is one more answer to identity that is increasingly elusive.

Conclusion

THOUGHTS ON THE REDISCOVERY OF SELF

Did anyone really think things would turn out otherwise—that the massive, global kinship dislocations of the past sixty years *wouldn't* produce increasingly visible, transformative effects not only in individual lives and households, but on politics and culture too?

"Destroying the family life of highly social, intelligent animals leads inevitably to misery among individual survivors and pathological misbehavior among the group," J. M. Coetzee, recipient of the Nobel Prize for Literature, has explained.[1] He was speaking of elephants, of course. Recent years have seen an outpouring of concern around the globe about what G. A. Bradshaw, a psychologist and ecologist, and his colleagues have named "elephant breakdown."[2] Across Africa, India, and parts of Southeast Asia, the disruption of elephant families via poaching and other human interventions has led to massive interruptions of social learning, stark increases in aberrant behavior, and trauma and stress.

So, as just indicated, the depletion of a critical mass of older males has given rise to rampaging behavior by young males—behavior that does not exist when older bulls are there, because their mere presence keeps younger bulls in social line.[3] Young females taken from their mothers and allomothers turn out to lack maternal skills themselves, because they were unable to learn them in community.[4] Animals in decimated herds exhibit the same traits as humans diagnosed with trauma disorder: "abnormal startle response, unpredictable asocial behavior, inattentive mothering and aggression." Some young bulls have so lost their sense of elephant-ness that they have taken to raping rhinos.

As Bradshaw summarizes, decades of serious insults to the elephants' environment "have so disrupted the intricate web of familial and societal relations by which young elephants have traditionally been raised in the wild, and by which established elephant herds are governed, that what we are now witnessing is nothing less than a precipitous collapse of elephant culture."[5]

The elephants, one might conclude, are undergoing a massive crisis of identity, brought about by environmental shattering of the families and societies that have hitherto made them the animals they are. *Homo sapiens* may not be in crisis on the same scale as the mighty pachyderms of Africa and Asia. But shouldn't it be possible to share in the solicitude for these distressed animals and see that there might be a point or two of connection between their social predicament and our own? To do otherwise is to engage in speciesism at its most perverse.

Again, one needn't assume a crude reductionism, or one-to-one correspondence, to understand that massive disturbances in the human ecosystem are affecting individuals all over the place, and in different unpredictable ways. As René Girard's theory of social contagion indicates, communal creatures like human beings respond to collective signals. This brings us to perhaps the deepest problem with identity politics: the collective signals to which identitarians respond are increasingly incoherent. Identity has become a forever war whose combatants now habitually turn on their own in a spiral of scapegoating and social destruction that no one seems to know how to stop.

Consider an example that materialized in March 2019, captured in a *New York Times* piece called "Teen Fiction and the Perils of Cancel Culture."[6] It reported the case a young black man who identified as gay and was employed as a "sensitivity reader" by various publishing houses. In that capacity, he enforced "cancel culture" (i.e., the flagging of material that progressive groupthink would deem unacceptable). As he once explained those standards on Twitter, "Stories about the civil rights movement should be written by black people, Stories of suffrage should be written by women. . . . Why is this so hard to get?" So far, so unremarkable for the politics of appropriation.

Then he wrote and tried to publish a book of his own. The result, as the story puts it, was a "karmic boomerang." For although the protagonists of his story were teenagers who fit the race and sex qualifications of his supposed cultural bailiwick, his secondary characters were not. They were Serbs and Albanians. The author made the catastrophic mistake, by identitarian standards, of situating some of his story in Kosovo's civil war in the late 1990s. Following a Twitter storm in which he was disparaged for focusing on people of privilege and being insensitive to Muslims, he withdrew his debut book before circulation. As the reporter summarized, "He was Robespierre with his own neck in the cradle of the guillotine."

This is one of many stories signaling the uniquely destructive power of identity politics—specifically, its power to destroy *its own*. There are the feminists who were once included within progressive ranks, only to be shunned permanently for excommunicable offenses—like opining that allowing biological males to compete in female sports will undermine female athletes. These have included one of the greatest female athletes of the modern era, tennis legend Martina Navratilova.[7] The same fate has visited other transgressors who have lagged evolving identity commandments by only a step or two, like novelist Ian McEwan and feminist grande dame Germaine Greer.[8] Many other luminaries have now run afoul of "cancel culture" enforcers. Identity politics has become a tale of two, three, many Dantons, and its tumbrils will not stop rolling until other ways of answering *Who am I?* return, or are recovered.

The crisis over identity is part and parcel of a larger unraveling. As mentioned at the outset, foreboding saturates the politics and societies of the West today. Surely at least some of it is emanating from human beings who know that *something* potentially serious is afoot, but who are still searching for the differential diagnosis. It is not impossible to hear in today's secular jeremiads a displaced panic for a pandemic no one saw coming: the diminution of the human story itself.

Some of the best writing of our time is precisely that which worries over the civilizational sap of the West.[9] All draw from the same profound wells of cultural disquiet. Maybe, deep down, Western men and women are right to be afraid—right to fear the future, right to apprehend that somewhere along the way, *Homo sapiens* really has gone and done something harmful to itself.

Friedrich Nietzsche famously predicted that it would take "hundreds and hundreds of years" for humanity to understand the death of God. It may take at least that many for the same humanity to face en masse an authentic reckoning of what it has wrought in living as if we are different creatures than we are, liberated from needs that ineradicably make us what we are. Maybe what the childless, prophetic Nietzsche professed to see in the "tombs" of European cathedrals wasn't quite what he took it to be. Maybe, instead of someone else's corpse, it was a self-inflicted wound.

But that wound is not the end of the story. As with any major shock to an ecosystem, winners and losers will emerge from the extraordinary transformation of the Western social order witnessed during the lifetimes of people reading this; in fact, they already have. Some of those winners—at least, temporary winners—could be seen in the #MeToo narratives. They show what other evidence shows: the sexual revolution has ushered in the age of Thrasymachus, who in Plato's *Republic* defined the best political order as rule by the strongest. The revolution further empowers the already strong and further undermines the already weak.[10]

Yet the return of Thrasymachus is not necessarily the end of the story either. The reassertion of communal nature may yet yield up new forms of self-defense.

It may someday turn out the "elites" and "nonelites" of the future, for example, are not defined as socioeconomically as they are today. Perhaps the real divide of postrevolutionary humanity lies between those who have figured out how to navigate the Great Scattering successfully and those who have not. Such might seem to be the nascent meaning, for example, of a phenomenon that sociologists W. Bradford Wilcox and Wendy Wang have documented in detail: the "class divide" over marriage, meaning that people in better-off classes are more likely to be married than are others.[11]

This split has given rise to the seeming puzzle of "talking left" but "living right," as American meritocracy has produced families at the top of the socioeconomic ladder that avoid divorce and single parenthood—even as many of their members tend toward the more progressive end of politics. Maybe this is not a puzzle after all. Maybe these people are harbingers, early beneficiaries of an enhanced understanding of what makes for human thriving—even if their ideological opinions lag their successful social adaptation. And quite aside from itinerant sociological patterns, a wider renorming or other awakening, great or no, may yet rise up from a future reckoning of what damage to the human environment has wrought.

Meanwhile, other men and women surveying today's social chaos might join the emerging moral counterculture in growing numbers—say, via the Benedict Option urged by Rod Dreher or in related ways of constructing postrevolutionary lives that self-consciously return to a time before so many forgot who they are.[12] It is interesting, for instance, that within American Catholicism, the most vibrant orders and lay movements—the ones that gain converts—lean toward orthodoxy.[13] The same is true of American Protestantism, for reasons that sociologists have explained.[14] The human animals who hear and act on such contrarian but powerful cues may yet turn out to hit upon the most successful postrevolutionary strategy of all.

Ultimately, this argument over identity politics and its origins concerns anthropology more than it does politics. This means, among other consequences, that a seemingly obligatory "what is to be done?" finale is here omitted.

Even so, one closing political irony is certain. While attention to identity politics has become the object of conversation mostly in the left-leaning circles of American and English and European political thought, deliverance from today's disfigurations will not—and cannot—come from that same quarter.

The reason is simple: not only identitarians, but also liberals and progressives who are now anti-identitarian or identitarian-skeptical, all agree on one big thing, at least so far: the sexual revolution is social bedrock—off-limits for revision intellectually, morally, and politically. No-fault divorce, out-of-wedlock births, paid surrogacy, absolutism about erotic freedom, disdain for traditional religious codes: the very policies and practices that have chipped away at the family, and helped to provoke the subsequent flight to identity politics, are those that liberals and progressives embrace.

Then there are related social realities that left-liberalism also deems benign, and that also put a dent on familial identity. Pornography—which once upon a time some feminists thought to object to—is now the stuff of tony enthusiasm. Prostitution is being redefined by progressives around the West as anodyne "sex work." And, of course, abortion—in the unnerving theological modifier often applied by in the liberal-progressive coalition—remains what they call "sacrosanct." As a political matter, asking liberals and progressives to solve the problem of identity politics is like asking the orphan with chutzpah to find out who murdered his parents.

Yes, conservatives and other nonprogressives have missed something major about identity politics: its authenticity. But the liberal-progressive side has missed something bigger. Identity politics is not so much politics as a primal scream. It's the result of the Great Scattering—our species' unprecedented collective retreat from our very selves.

Anyone who has ever heard a coyote in the desert, separated at night from its pack, knows the sound. The otherwise unexplained hysteria of today's identity politics is nothing more, or less, than just that: the collective human howl of our time, sent up by inescapably communal creatures trying desperately to identify their own.

PART TWO

COMMENTARY

Rod Dreher

In recent decades, it has become fashionable among historians to deride the view that the fifth-century collapse of the Roman Empire in the West was a civilizational catastrophe. We are no longer allowed to call the Germanic tribes who overthrew Rome "barbarians," nor are we permitted to describe the first centuries after Rome's demise a "Dark Age."

This is misleading. No doubt the standard Enlightenment-era view that fierce tribes overthrew a great and glorious civilization that had grown weak and decadent needed some revision. However, leaving aside contentious cultural judgments about Rome's fall, there can be no doubt that it was an unprecedented material disaster. In his 2005 book *The Fall Of Rome And The End Of Civilization*, Oxford historian Bryan Ward-Perkins cites extensive archaeological evidence that Western Europe suffered an astounding loss of the material basis for its culture when Rome and its complex economy collapsed.

We don't know precisely why Rome's postimperial economy fell apart, but the evidence that it did is undeniable. People forgot how to do things. They forgot how to read and write. They forgot how to rotate crops. They forgot how to smelt iron. It took Western Europeans six or seven centuries to relearn how to build a roof as well as Romans did. There was an immense amount of poverty and suffering in post-Roman western Europe. It may be politically incorrect to say so, but Ward-Perkins commonsensically concludes that he would never want to endure the kinds of horrors that were common then.

Fair enough, but so what? Nobody today actually argues for a return to the rusticity of early medieval European life. Ward-Perkins is so emphatic about his dissenting scholarship because he worries that we don't take civilization's fragility seriously enough. He writes: "Romans before the fall were as certain as we are today that their world would continue forever substantially unchanged. They were wrong. We would be wise not to repeat their complacency."[1]

The urbanist Jane Jacobs shares Ward-Perkins's alarm. In her final book, 2004's *Dark Age Ahead,* Jacobs argues vigorously that despite our immense wealth and technological sophistication, we in the modern West are courting catastrophe. She describes a Dark Age as a period of "mass amnesia," in which "the previous way of life slides into an abyss of forgetfulness, almost as decisively as if it had never existed."[2]

One of the clear signs of our impending Dark Age, says Jacobs, is that we have "families rigged to fail."[3] She says that family and, by extension, community, is one of the pillars on which a civilized social order stands. Weak families mean weak communities, which in turn means a weak civilization. Today, Jacobs writes, we have constructed a society that makes it harder to form and sustain families. The failure of the late Roman family contributed to the feebleness of the Empire and left it vulnerable to destruction. So it is with us, says Jacobs.

Why did Rome fall? Ask five scholars, get six answers. One key factor, however, was the decline of the family. In his unjustly forgotten 1940s-era study *Family and Civilization*, Harvard sociologist Carle C. Zimmerman traces the connection between family systems and civilizational decline from ancient Greece to imperial Rome to the modern era.

In Zimmerman's telling, Rome's familial system began to crack in the second and third centuries, with the rise of a more individualistic ethic. Historical records show that many of the same social phenomena familiar to us in the twenty-first century—high divorce rates, declining fertility, mainstreaming sexual diversity, and "positive social antagonism to the old domestic family system and the family among the whole masses of people"[4]—were all present in Rome during its final decline.

Crucially, Zimmerman says these are not causes of decline, but rather outward symptoms of a decadent inner condition. Society is held together by families, he contends, and families by *fides* and *sacramentum*—that is, loyalty (*fides*) in relationships and a shared conviction that those relationships, especially the family, are anchored in religious belief (*sacramentum*), or at least in transcendent values.

Familism—a way of life that holds the needs of the family to be superior to those of the individual—cannot succeed "without a system of infinite faith, which is simply the acceptance of a basic code of values."[5] The clan model of family relations crushes the individual and eventually gives way to the "domestic" model, which balances the needs of the collective with the needs of the individual. But individualism dilutes the domestic model, creating the "atomistic" family—what we today call the "nuclear" family.

In Zimmerman's account, the atomistic family system causes

the loss of religious belief that all family systems require to exist. This critical insight was brought to stunning new life in Mary Eberstadt's 2013 book, *How the West Really Lost God*. Societies that lose the family also lose the faith, and vice versa.[6] They enter into an age of chaos and darkness until they rediscover the value of familism—and the cycle starts again.

None of these three are religious thinkers per se, though Ward-Perkins and Zimmerman openly acknowledge that their pessimism goes against the prevailing values of their time and intellectual class. Though religious rebirth may be the only real hope for our civilization, Christians in the contemporary world should not be under the illusion that they are immune from the loss of faith and familism.

Until I read *Primal Screams*, I had not connected the destructive rage of identity politics with the terror quite understandably produced by the disintegration of society, of community, of family, and even, as we now see, of the self. The Great Scattering, as Eberstadt calls it, is a diabolical thing, fundamentally connected to the loss of religion.

Though the theological dimension of this claim is obvious, here I'm speaking etymologically. The words "diabolic" and "symbolic" are related. "Symbol" comes from the Greek words meaning "to throw together"; "diabolic" can be understood as its antonym. Something diabolic is an agent that divides, in an adversarial way. Note also that the word "religion" comes from the Latin word *religare*, which means "to bind together."

This is not simply a clever word game. The future of our civilization is at stake. Reading Eberstadt in light of these other thinkers, it becomes clear that in the modern West, we are simply forgetting the art of creating and sustaining families. Our technology and our wealth conceal the seriousness of the crisis, but make no mistake: if "barbarism" can be understood as a state of mass amnesia, in which we deny any sense of order outside of our own desires, then we are already living in a barbaric Dark Age.

We are not quite there yet—but we are fast running out of time. Identity politics is not the cause of our calamity, but only the most acute symptom of it. As with late Rome, so with us: only the recovery of *fides* and *sacramentum* will right this sinking ship.

Though this is clearly not a crisis that will be solved by politics alone, politics must be part of the response. Conservatives must realize that the free market fundamentalism so many have embraced without question is inimical to family stability. Ask the people in Rust Belt communities what they think of the "creative destruction" valorized by the right. Ironically, the dissolution of families and communities necessarily means a greater social role for the welfare state.

In the Trump era, more and more conservatives are recognizing the role economics plays in social fragmentation and decline. Alas, progressives are not remotely near grasping how sexual libertinism is doing the same thing, and arguably worse. As Eberstadt observes, "The sexual revolution is bedrock—off-limits for revision intellectually, morally, and politically." The sexual revolution's propaganda is the prosperity gospel for progressives.

If only the answer were only a matter of going back to church! The problem is that most Americans' idea of Christianity has been watered down by radical individualism and a consumerist mentality. University of Notre Dame sociologist Christian Smith, a leading authority on the religious beliefs and practices of younger Americans, says that the de facto religion of the young Christians (and not only Christians) is something he calls "Moralistic Therapeutic Deism."[7] Moralistic Therapeutic Deism (MTD) is a pseudoreligion that inhabits the institutions and language of traditional faith, but hollows it out from inside.

MTD teaches that God is a cosmic butler who wants nothing

more than for us all to be happy, self-fulfilled, and nice to others. It is the perfect religion for bourgeois consumers, offering them psychological assurance and emotional validation without having to change or accommodate themselves to difficult teachings. According to Smith, MTD "is about attaining subjective well-being, being able to resolve problems, and getting along amiably with other people." At best, says Smith, MTD is a "pathetic" version of Christianity; at worst, "Christianity is actively being colonized and displaced by a quite different religious faith."[8]

This matters because if the recovery of religion is necessary to civilizational regeneration, then it cannot be tepid modern forms of the faith. Liberal Protestantism and progressive Catholicism have already made their peace with the sexual revolution, and signs are that this accommodation is spreading more generally within Christianity. It's poison. Whatever theological case might be made for liberal Christianity, from a familism point of view, it amounts to being stranded on a savage shore and burning the boats that would have been one's only means of escape.

I was grateful to read Mary Eberstadt's mention of the Benedict Option as a countercultural survival strategy for this new Dark Age.[9] I came up with the idea based on the life and teachings of St. Benedict of Nursia (480-547), the founder of Western monasticism. Benedict was born four years after the barbarian chief Odoacer deposed the final Western Roman emperor. Benedict arrived in the city of Rome to complete his education, but was so shocked by the chaos and decadence he saw there that he turned his back to the fallen imperial capital and set out for the forest.

Eventually Benedict came to lead monasteries and to write his famous Rule, a simple guide for how to live together in disciplined vowed community. When he died in 547, Benedict left behind twelve monasteries in Rome's vicinity and the mother house at Monte Cassino. Benedictine monasticism spread like wildfire across the tinder of early medieval Europe, offering light, order, learning, and hope in a time when all those things were exceedingly rare. Five centuries later, there were thousands of monasteries scattered across western Europe. The Benedictines had laid the groundwork for the recovery of civilization.

Benedict is a saint for our time. He emerged from the wreckage of a great civilization whose spiritual and moral energies had been widely scattered. Benedict gathered. Though meant for monks, his Rule is a model of *fides* and *sacramentum*—of living in sacred commitment to God and to one's community, all bound to and through a system of infinite faith and the preservation of cultural memory. They dwelled together as a sign of contradiction to the dissolute way of the world. The memory of civilization crossed the dark and stormy sea of the early medieval era within the ark of the monasteries.

In the twenty-first century, lay Christians of all confessions can—and must—learn from the Benedictines. What else is there? As Mary Eberstadt's *Primal Screams* makes clear to this reader, for those who want to endure the Great Scattering, the Benedict Option is not a choice, but a mandate.

Mark Lilla

Mary Eberstadt's *Primal Screams* is not easy reading. Nor is it meant to be. As in previous books, she sheds a klieg light on our children's lives that is not flattering for us, their parents. Why, she asks, are our children so unhappy? Why are more of them killing themselves in their teens and early twenties? Why, too, are so many obese, on prescription drugs, and in need of therapy? They have few siblings and fewer friends than children in previous generations; it seems they are also having less sex, whether because coupling has gotten too easy, or too hard because litigious, or too scary or because they are, so to speak, bowling alone, thanks to the Internet. Why too do increasing numbers seem unsure about their genders? Is it because they are finally free to choose? Or is it because their selves have trouble congealing in an increasingly fluid world?

These are all important questions that too many of my fellow liberals, for all their calls to "save the children," prefer not to contemplate for fear of having to reckon with the costs of their choices. (And I include myself.) Conservatives, to their credit, have taken these unsettling developments more to heart.

But they do not stop there and that, I'm afraid, is the problem. Their inquiries into social problems like these very quickly turn into indictments, if not inquisitions. Today's conservatives, like those in the past, are addicted to narratives of decline. And they have several versions to choose from today: the narrative that traces all social problems back to the 1960s, the one that blames the rise of liberalism, the one that blames secularism, the one that blames modernity *tout court*, and so on. The most convincing one to me has always been the one that traces our woes back to choices made in Eden. But it's hard to mobilize people politically to fight a sin we are all guilty of. Politics demands serpents.

Conservatives who are doing serious work on the state of our societies underestimate how much the just-so stories they atavistically return to end up limiting their audience. If pathology X proves the decline thesis, as does pathology Y, as does pathology Z, even the sympathetic listener will begin to wonder whether the inquirer is not just suffering from a fatal case of confirmation bias and stop listening. When a larger thesis gets in the way of an important finding, it is best to bracket that thesis out for a while and hold the finding up for examination from all sides, like a crystal. Doing that might open new lines of inquiry, and of communication, leading to a series of little but convincing insights. The impulse to pull those insights into a single big one—to place experience under a concept, as Kant put it—is irresistible to the human mind. But the longer we can hold out, the better.

Primal Screams advances two theses, one convincing, the other less so, to my mind. The smaller thesis—that young people's obsession with personal identity is linked somehow to their family troubles—is important. And it is a helpful corrective to the argument I advanced in *The Once and Future Liberal*, which traces how the liberal consensus established during what I call the "Roosevelt dispensation" degenerated into divisive cultural identity politics during the "Reagan dispensation" that recently ended with the election of Donald Trump.[1] As a consequence, I argued, liberals have been unable to develop an expansive vision of our shared national destiny, which is why they remain incapable of seizing durable power from an increasingly radical Republican party. A new approach, I concluded, is needed.

Mary Eberstadt, in an incisive review in the *Weekly Standard*, accepted my basic narrative, but pointed out that I had only accounted for the *supply* side of identity politics: that is, how a wider liberal vision became refracted into distinct claims by uncompromising identity groups. What I failed to account for was the *demand* side: why it is that so many young people today find this identity politics attractive and in some sense nourishing. This is because, she argues, they are suffering from the "breakdown of the American family," a term she explains in the text you've read. I think there is a great deal to this. What I called somewhat hyperbolically a "pseudo-politics of self-regard" fits well with her analysis of the narcissistic personality traits that more and more of our children are displaying.

I would even go further, now that I've read her. I think we might also interpret the attraction to defining oneself in terms of predetermined identity categories as an awkward attempt to connect with others—an escape attempt from the atomized, unstable world those in modern society find themselves in. I saw identity politics as an expression of the individualistic ideology of our time; it might also provide an effort to exit one's shell, though on one's own terms. Yes, our children may be craving more order in their lives and certainly need it. But they are also being taught by everything in our culture that they shouldn't feel bound by anything given. Affinities must remain elective and cancelable at any time. Which hardly provides the security and reliability of family.

So this first thesis I accept: the vogue for identity politics bears some relation to the atomization and fragility of family life today. It is the second thesis—which traces that atomization back to the sexual revolution—that I find unconvincing. All narratives that focus on a single cultural moment as a decisive break in history risk falling into a classic logical fallacy: *post hoc ergo propter hoc*, whatever follows an event is caused by that event. Pessimistic theories of historical decline almost always fall into this error. The narrator thinks that the more effects he can trace back to the cause, the more convincing his account will be; but just the opposite is the case. The more weight a historical event is made to bear, the less it really explains. And the less it offers a guide to future action.

Let's consider a more encompassing thesis than the one Mary Eberstadt puts forward. Let's posit that the sexual revolution, the atomization of our families, and identity politics—all real, all problematic—are actually effects of larger, long-term historical forces now at work more globally. One effect didn't cause the others; consider in longer historical perspective, they all happened simultaneously. Consider two such forces.

The first is wealth and what usually comes with wealth, *embourgeoisement*. It is hard to grasp the tremendous revolution in human societies—and, I would say, human psychology—brought about in our lifetimes by prosperity and technology. Mary Eberstadt idealizes the life of "the illiterate peasant of the Middle Ages," whose life was shorter but supposedly more meaningful because he lived in a tighter web of human relations. Fewer and fewer people anywhere in the world are leading such lives or want to. And fewer and fewer will be in the future. It's over. Global prosperity is bringing with it middle-class tastes and demands, and sometimes traditionally aristocratic ones (such as sexual promiscuity).

Among those demands is the desire to control family size, which turns out to be universal once it can be satisfied. We once needed high birthrates to survive given higher mortality and the demands of agricultural life. Now that this is no longer the case, people want to choose, which is why they have embraced the Pill, prophylactics, and abortion around the world. People are highly aware of the tradeoff between family size and the resources available to each member, including themselves, and now have the power to determine the balance. A *Washington Post* article that happened to be published while I was writing this response bears out the point.[2] One Beijing mother interviewed remarked, "If we have a second child and our business is not good, our quality of our life will go down, and I won't be able to offer such good things for both of them. . . . Plus, it will be harder for me to go to work with two." This belief has absolutely nothing to do with the sexual revolution, which is the only revolution that seems to have passed China, and much of East Asia, by. It has everything to do with now being able to choose and having more middle-class tastes determine that choice.

This is not to say that the decision to have smaller families is a wise one. Yes, there are more resources for each child, but how good is it for them to grow up without siblings or cousins? This is a problem we need to face in the future, and efforts at education and persuasion are more likely to move people than jeremiads. It is striking how quickly Chinese families today have developed many of the pathologies that Mary Eberstadt complains about in the West: delayed marriage, spoiled single children who spend all their time on-line rather than socializing or playing with siblings, difficulty with sexual relations, and so forth. Not long ago, this country once known for its veneration of ancestors had to pass a law guaranteeing grandparents visiting rights to see their grandchildren. All these developments reinforce Mary Eberstadt's first thesis about family breakdown more generally but weaken the second one tracing it all back to the sexual revolution.

The second larger force that is more likely responsible for the social changes that disturb her is what the Polish sociologist Zygmunt Bauman called the "liquidity" of contemporary life, and in particular the supercharged capitalism of our time—something that, to my astonishment and disappointment, she only sees fit to mention obliquely in one sentence. (Another conservative bad habit, I'm afraid.) Marx wrote dramatically that under capitalism "all that's solid melts into air," as social institutions are created and destroyed over and over again. Bauman argues that given the speed of economic, technological, and informational change under contemporary capitalism, social institutions melt but they never resolidify into new ones. Rather, the lifespan of more and more institutions keeps shrinking while the lifespan of human beings keeps increasing. That is why everything seems so liquid, always moving, leaving nowhere fixed to stand: fewer of the institutions that existed when we were born are still there when we die. Consequently, people feel tremendous disquiet, since we are creatures who need solid institutions and solid human relationships. One of Bauman's books is even titled *Liquid Love*.[3]

Bauman's thesis sheds some interesting light both on my argument regarding the individualism behind identity politics and Mary Eberstadt's thesis regarding family breakdown. It also forces us to think harder about how we might cope with both developments. Conservatives want to combat social liquidity while celebrating economic liquidity; liberals do the reverse. We have yet to see a coherent ideology that addresses both problems simultaneously—though my impression is that a lot of contemporary political agitation that is being classed as populist expresses a desire for a less liquid world more generally. More stable institutions, more stable economies, more stable populations, even more stable genders. But how to bring that about decently? When I think of our contemporary situation, I am reminded of the story of an old man on his first rail journey, who tried to stop the train by pulling on the seat in front of him.

We need to think about all this lucidly. Americans are subject to panic attacks—especially concerning anything related to sex—and are prone to ring alarms, which only contributes to the panic. Tocqueville saw right through us when he spent just a year here a long time ago. But he was mainly addressing the panic of a French aristocracy that thought all democracies end in the Terror. He calmly explained to them that the West had entered a new historical phase, that a new regime was ascendant and needed to be understood in its own terms, both for the benefits it could bring and the dangers it posed. And because it was inevitable. We could use more of that spirit today.

Peter Thiel

Mary Eberstadt traces the rise of the new woke religion of identity politics to the same cause she had previously found for the decline of traditional faith: family breakdown. For Eberstadt, the crisis of our time is a crisis of the family.

Eberstadt is correct to point out that religious belief is not a matter of context-free choice, since it begins in the home. I would add that family formation is not a matter of context-free choice, since it rests on an economic base. Every family needs an income to pay for home, school, and hospital: from the bill for giving birth; through monthly payments for a house that combines living space, job proximity, and school access; on up to tuition for a diploma from a more or less dubious college. And for decades now, the economic preconditions for family formation have been moving in the wrong direction. Incomes have been stagnant while health care, education, and housing get more expensive every year.

This fundamental fact of stagnation indicates that the crisis of our time is not just a crisis of the family. It is a crisis of the future. Looking back at the modern West of the last three centuries, one can define the middle class as all those who expected their children to do better than themselves. This belief thrived on the frontier, so it was only natural that America had larger families and more religion than Europe in the nineteenth century. When the frontier in the United States began to close toward the end of the nineteenth century, power shifted to the more zero-sum large cities of the East Coast. By the time of the relatively secular 1930s, America was much closer to Europe. The Great Depression brought a collapse in expectations about the future and a demographic collapse in the number of children.

There was a partial reopening of a new frontier in the post-1945 years through the automobile, suburbanization, and the construction of the highway system. This happened in both Europe and the United States but was larger and more sustained in the United States. The demographic slowdown began post-1964, with the rise of environmentalism and ever more restrictive zoning laws generally. Perhaps as important as the Pill was Jane Jacobs' signature victory over Robert Moses in 1962: she preserved Greenwich Village against a proposed highway, but she set New York on a decades-long arc toward ever more expensive housing. The global megacities and their prosperous hinterlands like Malibu, Marin, and New Canaan became bulwarks of hostility to family formation. Causes like "neighborhood character" and "biodiversity" provided idealistic fig leaves for a retreat from common prosperity.

A form of suburbanization continued in the United States during the long boom of 1982–2007, when U.S. demographics and religiosity continued to look much healthier than Europe's. But what followed in the crisis of 2008 was a negative watershed moment for families especially. The housing bubble of the 2000s, in retrospect, appears as a "suburban and exurban" bubble—a last bubble of American exceptionalism, as it were—marking a collapse in the frontier-like growth expectations of suburban America from 1945 onward.

Eberstadt has rightly pointed to the crisis of the family. The resolution of that crisis will require nothing less than a broad reacceleration of American expectations about the future. Without such a reacceleration, Millennials face a much harder path than the Baby Boomers. This harder path is not more motivational. Declining expectations for the future act in a similar way to rising marginal tax rates, and one thing the free market economists are right about is that substitution effects dominate income effects. The worse future expectations get, the more people will substitute leisure for work, including the work of building families. The relatively stagnant economy means that such leisure will be relatively cheap things like yoga, marijuana, video games, and so on.

Identity politics itself functions as a cheap substitute for economic progress. Wall Street, Hollywood, and the Ivy League all find identity politics particularly congenial: for these pillars of the establishment, it is an economical way to appear more dynamic than they really are. Adding "diverse" directors to corporate boards, "diverse" directors to film crews, and "diverse" undergraduates to elite campuses (though they are more likely to come from prosperous immigrant families than from less well-off households of whatever shade) is cheap. It is also easier, and less threatening to incumbent elites, than structural reform of a stagnant economy that left the middle class behind long ago.

Afterword

My thanks to Rod Dreher, Mark Lilla, and Peter Thiel for engaging with the argument of this book. They demonstrate by way of example what a riven society needs most: civil, sincere discussion by people from diverse points of view. Though a brief afterword cannot do justice to all of their intriguing observations, I would like to comment here on a few of the most noteworthy.

Rod Dreher reminds us of something profound: we human beings forget, and not only the small stuff. As he notes, Bryan Ward-Perkins' work on the Roman Empire and its aftermath of illiteracy in numerous realms is an excellent case in point. And those postcollapse Romans were not alone. The world is littered with the rubble of civilizations forgotten by generations who came later. Without such forgetting, archeology wouldn't need to exist. Shelley's poem "Ozymandias" is poignant not on account of the statue's arrogant inscription, but because no one reading it remembers the mighty king, or his kingdom, anymore.

And so it is today. Post-sexual revolution, we have forgotten something that other social animals never need to be reminded of: that we require others of our kind for understanding who we are; and that without such connection, we are blind and mute—sometimes literally.

The entire world received a relevant lesson in "attachment theory" only a few decades ago, when the severe deprivation within Romanian orphanages of the 1980s was exposed following the fall of Communism. Unable to bond with adults, child victims suffered all manner of distress born of such emotional indigence—self-harm, psychiatric problems, and smaller brains among them. These results, like those of Harlow's deprived rhesus monkeys, exist at one end of a spectrum. The rising mental instability of younger Western generations—captured often in statistics and incarnate in the often-irrational public expression of identity politics—surely falls somewhere on the same line.

Dreher is also on the mark in observing that "if the recovery of religion is necessary to civilizational regeneration, then it cannot be tepid modern forms of the faith." No one builds a Chartres or a Sagrada Familia for Moralistic Therapeutic Deism (MTD). No one even gets out of bed for MTD on Sunday—or any other day. The churches that have made their peace with the sexual revolution, as Dreher observes and as I argued in *How the West Really Lost God*, will soon be churches no more.

Mark Lilla's contribution, like his book *The Once and Future Liberal*, enters critical territory of a different kind. It's to be hoped that others on the liberal-left will follow his independent lead and enter into conversation with nonleftists in the name of the public good.

We agree on one big thing, as Lilla writes: "The attraction to defining oneself in terms of predetermined identity categories [is] an awkward attempt to connect with others —an escape attempt from the atomized, unstable world those in modern society find themselves in." This is vital, and true. It signals what has been missing in discussions of identity politics to date, especially by those outside such politics: empathy, including for those who gravitate toward group identities because they cannot find their "selves" anywhere else.

Beyond that comity, Lilla sorts our differences into standard categories of left/right, liberal/conservative, and so forth. This is understandable shorthand; we all use it. At the same time, I wonder whether these binaries remain adequate to the phenomenon of identity politics, whose origins appear to be *pre*political.

The new violence on campuses and elsewhere amounts more to a madness of crowds than it does to political speech. And that same unbound irrationalism is now exiling and stigmatizing more and more *anti*-irrationalists, wherever they come from. Though it's beyond the purview of this book, it seems clear that society stands in dire need of a coalition of the reasonable, irrespective of location on the political spectrum. Maybe this closing can be a start.

On the critical side, Lilla contests the book's argument about the centrality of the sexual revolution in this volatile new mix of identitarianism and attendant anxieties. His argument is classic: a quasi-Hegelian insistence that capital-H history has its inexorable ways, and that the rest of humanity needs to face that fact and get over it.

But there are specters stalking the idea of inexorability. They include the examples of other social phenomena that were once thought to be inevitable, yet are no more. Half a century ago, tobacco smoking was ubiquitous, including in airplanes and some hospital rooms. Collectively convinced by evidence about harm, Western societies drew stricter boundaries around the practice. The same about-face has come to characterize other social developments that we now look back on with disbelief—from the gin alleys of pre-Victorian London hundreds of years ago to the casual, lethal dispensing of opioids in the United States during the 1990s and into the 2010s.

Why should the sexual revolution, alone among all phenomena in history, be immune to second thoughts? After all, evidence already shows that it isn't. Raised after the invention of the sonogram machine, younger generations of Americans are already more prolife than their parents—and growing more so. Lilla is certainly correct that humanity around the world has embraced the ability to control the means of reproduction. But that evidence is not as dispositive as many believe—because other evidence pointing in a different social direction also abounds.

Recall the shocking data about loneliness and isolation in old age. Many of today's Western elderly seldom have visitors; some no longer have anyone to call them by their first names. Many Western young people, as also seen, are wracked with psychiatric and other problems brought on by social and familial atomization. Under stresses like these, aren't some kind of second thoughts *themselves* inevitable? Capital-H history may write off these and other casualties as so much collateral damage. Humanity, on the other hand, may ultimately prove less indifferent, and more concerned.

Peter Thiel makes the point that we face not only a crisis of the family, but a crisis of the future. He is surely right to highlight the radical change in the American middle class, now uncertain about whether its children will do better than their parents did. The unprecedented decline in life expectancy, cited earlier, underscores the point.

As noted in the introduction, multiple social and economic factors are converging in America's disarray. As Thiel observes, these include the crash of 2008, from which many of the

Millennials' home-owning parents have yet to recover, and the staggering rise in student loan debt, also falling heaviest on the shoulders of the young. These adverse developments unrelated to the sexual revolution have doubtless left indelible marks. So, one assumes, have other epochal events that transpired when today's undergraduates were children: 9/11, followed by wars in Iraq and Afghanistan.

Thiel also illuminates a phenomenon that has not been well understood: the commercial exploitation of today's anxiety over identity—specifically in the form of "virtue-signaling" by corporations. Such theater is not only cheap in the sense of being cheesy. As he points out, it is also cheaper economically than anything else corporate actors might do—like thinking through creative solutions to the problem of student debt, say, or of devising alternatives to an overheated college market. Sensible people need to understand Hollywood's and corporate America's preening. It is an economically self-interested action, and it deserves calling out.

We cannot understand the Western crisis over identity without also understanding the forces he names—especially the fact that "for decades now, the economic preconditions for family formation have been moving in the wrong direction." At the same time, economics is not the fundament of what ails us. Too many earlier generations managed to construct families and communities with fewer resources than today's Americans. The veterans who returned from World War II to three-bedroom homes in Levittown were not materially better off than middle-class people today—far from it—but they married and had families of size anyway. Nor were they alone. Across the societies of the Western world, the 1950s were marked simultaneously by a baby boom and a religious boom. Both began decelerating, and then changing direction, after the early 1960s.

In the end, it seems reasonable to conclude that among its

other fallout, the simultaneous collapse of family and faith has now given rise to one more unforeseen consequence, the omnipresent craving for identity.

The problem that leaves us with is plain enough: Western politics is increasingly transformed by deep emotions that lie outside of politics itself. What to do about this moving yet destructive dynamic is among the most pressing issues of our time. It's the joint hope of this author, and of the book's contributors, that we have set out some parameters for a wider and necessary public conversation to come.

Acknowledgments

This book began in a meeting over coffee in 2017 with Robert Messenger, who was then an editor at the *Weekly Standard*. As a result of his encouragement, my essay on "The Primal Scream of Identity Politics" appeared in the magazine later that year. I'm grateful for his early confidence in the idea, and to the late *Weekly Standard* for publishing the piece.

Susan Arellano, head of Templeton Press, has now been the instrument of two of my books: this one, and *How the West Really Lost God* (2013). She is an exemplary editor and friend, and my debt to her is as great as my admiration. The rest of the Templeton team—Angelina Horst, Dan Reilly, and Trish Vergilio—have been a pleasure to work with, as before. Thanks, too, to Natalie Silver for her help with the text.

Robert Royal, head of the Faith and Reason Institute where I'm a senior fellow, has been a model of intellectual solidarity throughout the writing of this book. Two other friends improved the manuscript mightily along the way. Adam Keiper put an early version through the wringer, thereby stripping away many stains and blotches. Stanley Kurtz analyzed the text line by line for everything from verbal repetition to logical and historical consistency. I'm grateful to them for sparing the overall argument from its author's shortcomings.

Other comrades subjected in conversation to various aspects of the thesis include Ryan T. Anderson, Peter Atkinson, Mark Bauerlein, Mitchell Boersma, Andrew Ferguson, J. D. Flynn, Fr. Justin Huber, Fr. Dominic Legge, Rusty Reno, Cindy Searcy, Christopher White, and Fr. Thomas Joseph White. The Sarah B. Scaife Foundation has supported some of the work on this book, which would not have materialized without said help. I am grateful to Montgomery Brown for understanding not only this project, but also the line of reasoning developed in previous books as precursors. Thanks as well to Frank Hanna, and to Rob and Berni Neal, for encouraging my recent work.

Ideas percolate over time. Some thoughts in this book appeared in various essays, including in *National Review* ("Jailhouse Feminism," 2015) and *National Affairs* ("Two Nations, Revisited," 2018). Thanks to the editors in both for permission, and for allowing me to hammer out ideas in their pages. George Weigel and Stephen White, alongside the students of the Tertio Millennio Seminar in Krakow, Poland, have heard some of the ideas herein tried out during my annual talks in the program. I'm grateful as ever for their unique collective fellowship.

Thanks again to Rod Dreher, Mark Lilla, and Peter Thiel for their outstanding contributions to this book.

Putting first things last: Frederick, Catherine, Isabel, and Alexandra Eberstadt once again tolerated cheerfully the inconveniences of harboring a writer in the family. They had to; all of them are writers, too. So is their father. Like most children, ours will always wonder what it would have been like to have normal parents. Finally and as ever, my greatest earthly debt is to my husband and intellectual companion of decades, Nicholas Eberstadt, to whom this book is dedicated.

Notes

Introduction

1. Ben Zimmer, "The Phrase 'Lone Wolf' Goes Back Centuries," *Wall Street Journal*, December 19, 2014, https://www.wsj.com/articles/the-phrase-lone-wolf-goes-back-centuries-1419013651.

2. Temple Grandin and Catherine Johnson, *Animals Make Us Human: Creating the Best Life for Animals* (Boston: Mariner Books, 2009), 26.

3. Grandin and Johnson, *Animals Make Us Human*, 26.

4. "Coyote," Humane Society Wildlife Land Trust, http://www.wildlifelandtrust.org/wildlife/close-ups/coyote-wildlife-close-up.html.

5. Visala Kantamneni, "6 Animal Species with Strong Animal Bonds," *One Green Planet*, January 2019, https://www.onegreenplanet.org/animalsandnature/animal-species-with-strong-family-bonds/.

6. Charles Siebert, "An Elephant Crackup?," *New York Times Magazine*, October 8, 2006, https://www.nytimes.com/2006/10/08/magazine/an-elephant-crackup.html.

7. Liz Langley, "Can Cats Recognize Their Grandparents?,"

National Geographic, July 25, 2015, https://news.nationalgeographic
.com/2015/07/150725-animals-cats-science-recognition-family/.

8. M. J. Nelson-Flower et al., "The Lengths Birds Will
Go to Avoid Incest," *Journal of Animal Ecology* 81(2012): 735–37,
https://besjournals.onlinelibrary.wiley.com/doi/pdf/10.1111/j.1365
-2656.2012.02008.x.

9. Dustin R. Rubenstein and James Kealey, "Cooperation, Conflict, and the Evolution of Complex Animal Societies,"
Nature Education Knowledge 3, no. 10 (2010): 78, https://www.nature
.com/scitable/knowledge/library/cooperation-conflict-and-the
-evolution-of-complex-13236526.

10. C. van Schaik et al., "The Ecology of Social Learning in
Animals and Its Link with Intelligence," *Spanish Journal of Psychology*
19 (2017): E99, https://www.ncbi.nlm.nih.gov/pubmed/28065213.

11. Virginia Morell, "Do Animals Teach?," National Wildlife
Federation, September 28, 2015, https://nwf.org/Magazines
/National-Wildlife/2015/OctNov/Animals/Animal-Teaching.

12. Rachel Nuwer, "Mother Birds May Teach Their Chicks
to Sing before They Hatch," *Scientific American*, June 1, 2016,
https://www.scientificamerican.com/article/mother-birds-may
-teach-their-chicks-to-sing-before-they-hatch/.

13. Richard Pérez-Peña, "Elephants to Retire from Ringling
Brothers Stage," *New York Times*, March 5, 2015, https://www
.nytimes.com/2015/03/06/us/ringling-brothers-circus-dropping
-elephants-from-act.html.

14. Kristin Hugo, "Orca Shows and Breeding Banned in
California," *National Geographic*, September 14, 2016, https://news
.nationalgeographic.com/2016/09/california-bans-SeaWorld-orca
-breeding-entertainment/.

15. Aleksandra Pajda, "Yes! Mexico City Banned Captive
Dolphin Facilities," *One Green Planet*, April 2018, http://www.one
greenplanet.org/news/mexico-city-banned-captive-dolphin
-facilities/.

16. On stereotypies, see, for example, Lilly N. Edwards, "Animal
Well-Being and Behavioral Needs on the Farm," in *Improving Animal
Welfare: A Practical Approach*, ed. Temple Grandin (Boston: CABI, 2015),
https://www.grandin.com/inc/improving.animal.welfare.ch8.html.

17. Grandin and Johnson, *Animals Make Us Human*, 30.

18. Grandin and Johnson, *Animals Make Us Human*, chapter 1.

19. Alicia Kruisselbrink Flatt, "A Suffering Generation: Six Factors Contributing to the Mental Health Crisis in North American Higher Education," *College Quarterly* 16, no. 1 (2013), https://eric.ed.gov/?id=EJ1016492.

20. Betsy McKay, "U.S. Life Expectancy Falls Further," *Wall Street Journal*, November 29, 2018, https://www.wsj.com/articles/u-s-life-expectancy-falls-further-1543467660.

21. Melissa C. Mercado, Kristin Holland, and Ruth W. Leemis, "Trends in Emergency Department Visits for Nonfatal Self-Inflicted Injuries Among Youth Aged 10 to 24 Years in the United States, 2001-2015, *Journal of the American Medical Association* 318, no. 19 (2017): 1931–33, https://jamanetwork.com/journals/jama/article-abstract/2664031. Note, for example, that emergency room visits from females aged ten to fourteen rose a shocking 19 percent per year between 1999 and 2014.

22. Greg Jaffe and Jenna Johnson, "In America, Talk Turns to Something Not Spoken of for 150 Years: Civil War," *Washington Post*, March 2, 2019, https://www.washingtonpost.com/politics/in-america-talk-turns-to-something-unspoken-for-150-years-civil-war/2019/02/28/b3733af8-3ae4-11e9-a2cd-307b06d0257b_story.html?utm_term=.2c9bcdd21da4.

23. Kori Schake, "The End of the American Order," *Atlantic*, November 19, 2018, https://www.theatlantic.com/ideas/archive/2018/11/halifax-forum-allies-mourn-pre-trump-america/576154/.

24. Andrew Sullivan, "Democracies End When They Are Too Democratic," *New York*, May 1, 2016, http://nymag.com/intelligencer/2016/04/america-tyranny-donald-trump.html?gtm=bottom&gtm=top.

25. Elizabeth Drew, "Apocalypse Trump," *Project Syndicate*, December 24, 2018, https://www.project-syndicate.org/commentary/trump-syria-withdrawal-mattis-shutdown-by-elizabeth-drew-2018-12.

26. Roger Kimball, "The National Gallery of Identity Politics," *Wall Street Journal*, December 18, 2018, https://www.wsj.com/articles/the-national-gallery-of-identity-politics-11545179349.

27. Heather Mac Donald, "How Identity Politics Is Harming the Sciences," *City Journal*, Spring 2018, https://www.city-journal.org/html/how-identity-politics-harming-sciences-15826.html.

28. Rod Dreher, "Surviving the Woke Workplace," *American Conservative*, November 19, 2018, https://www.theamericanconservative.com/dreher/surviving-the-woke-workplace/.

29. Joe Conicha, "Tucker Carlson: 'Identity Politics Will Destroy This Country Faster Than a Foreign Invasion,'" *The Hill*, January 24, 2019, https://thehill.com/homenews/media/426747-tucker-carlson-identity-politics-will-destroy-this-country-faster-than-a.

30. Jordan Peterson Quotes (@JBPetersonQuote), "I don't like identity politics," Twitter, May 22, 2018, 4:30 p.m., https://twitter.com/jbpetersonquote/status/999039888258301952?lang=en.

31. Rod Dreher, "The Perils of Identity Politics," *American Conservative*, November 9, 2016, https://www.theamericanconservative.com/dreher/trump-perils-identity-politics/.

32. Michael Darer, "The Recent Spate of Anti-'Identity Politics' Hand-Wringing Is Proof That We Need Intersectionality More Than Ever," *HuffPost*, December 14, 2016, https://www.huffingtonpost.com/entry/the-recent-spate-of-anti-identity-politics-hand-wringing_us_5851ea52e4b0865ab9d4e910.

33. Mark Lilla, *The Once and Future Liberal: After Identity Politics* (New York: HarperCollins, 2017), 132–33.

34. Adam Rubenstein, "Steven Pinker: Identity Politics Is 'An Enemy of Reason and Enlightenment Values,'" *Weekly Standard*, February 15, 2018, https://www.weeklystandard.com/adam-rubenstein/steven-pinker-identity-politics-is-an-enemy-of-reason-and-enlightenment-values.

35. Robert D. Putnam, *Bowling Alone: The Collapse and Revival of American Community* (New York: Simon and Schuster, 2000).

36. This volume is also the final book-length piece of an intellectual exercise that I've been engaged in for several years now, trying to map just how much the sexual revolution has transformed the world.

My first book, *Home-Alone America*, looked logically to the largest body of literature then available on that subject—namely, the consequences to children and adolescents of the broken, typically fatherless, home. A few years later, *Adam and Eve after the Pill* examined other kinds of evidence indicating that the revolution was having paradoxical outcomes for men and women, and that it was also effecting a transvaluation of values on a Nietzschean scale as a humanity entranced with its promises struggled to square cultural circles that didn't exist before (Thus, for instance, the chapters titled "Is Food the New Sex?," "Is Pornography the New Tobacco?")

How the West Really Lost God, published in 2013, took the next logical step of analyzing how radical changes in the family were affecting secularization and altering religious beliefs and practices. It argued that contrary to conventional accounts of Christian decline, the contemporary emptying of the churches is due to the ways in which the sexual revolution has interrupted the transmission belt of religious learning itself. Following Ludwig Wittgenstein's observations about the impossibility of private language, I argued analogously that religion is practiced and learned, beginning in the social group of the family, and that disrupting this figurative classroom amounts to losing the "language" of faith itself.

The present book traces the fallout of these and other changes collectively, with particular focus on the increasingly searing questions of identity and identity politics.

37. Kristen Gelineau, "Mosque Shooter a White Nationalist Seeking Revenge," *Associated Press*, March 15, 2019, https://www .apnews.com/1e19fefcb2e948a1bf7ce63429bc186e.

38. Ben Smith, "Obama on Small-Town Pa.: Clinging to Religion, Guns, Xenophobia," *Ben Smith Blog, Politico*, April 11, 2008, https://www.politico.com/blogs/ben-smith/2008/04/obama-on -small-town-pa-clinging-to-religion-guns-xenophobia-007737.

39. For a representative analysis of such cases, see Mary Eberstadt, *It's Dangerous to Believe: Religious Freedom and Its Enemies* (New York: Harper, 2016). See also Rod Dreher, *The Benedict Option: A Strategy for Christians in a Post-Christian Nation* (New York: Penguin Random House, 2017).

40. Douglas Murray, *The Strange Death of Europe: Immigration, Identity, Islam* (London: Bloomsbury Continuum, 2017).

Chapter 1

1. Allan Bloom, *The Closing of the American Mind* (New York: Simon and Schuster, 1987).

2. Friedrich Nietzsche, *The Gay Science, Book III*, aphorism 193.

3. Bloom, *Closing*, 117.

4. Bloom, *Closing*, 118.

5. "1980s," Stanford Stories from the Archives, https://exhibits.stanford.edu/stanford-stories/feature/1980s.

6. Arthur Meier Schlesinger, Jr., *The Disuniting of America: Reflections on a Multicultural Society* (London: W. W. Norton, 1998) 22.

7. Todd Gitlin, *The Twilight of Common Dreams: Why America Is Wracked by Culture Wars* (New York: Holt, 1996).

8. Gitlin, *Twilight*.

9. Gitlin, *Twilight*.

10. Gitlin, *Twilight*, 215.

11. Bruce Bawer, *The Victims' Revolution: The Rise of Identity Studies and the Closing of the Liberal Mind* (New York: Broadside Books, 2012).

12. Judith Butler, quoted in Bawer, *Victims' Revolution*, 216.

13. "Identity Politics," *Stanford Encyclopedia of Philosophy*, March 23, 2016, https://www.google.com/search?client=safari&rls=en&q=stanford+encyclopedia+identity+politics&ie=UTF-8&oe=UTF-8.

14. Allison Stanger, "Understanding the Angry Mob at Middlebury That Gave Me a Concussion," *New York Times*, March 13, 2017, https://www.nytimes.com/2017/03/13/opinion/understanding-the-angry-mob-that-gave-me-a-concussion.html.

15. Tim Stanley, "Oxford Students Shut Down Abortion Debate: Free Speech Is Under Assault on Campus," *Telegraph*, November 19, 2014, https://www.telegraph.co.uk/news/politics /11239437/Oxford-students-shut-down-abortion-debate.-Free -speech-is-under-assault-on-campus.html.

16. Madison Park and Kyung Lah, "Berkeley Protests of Yiannopoulos Caused $100,000 in Damage," CNN, February 2, 2017, https://www.cnn.com/2017/02/01/us/milo-yiannopoulos -berkeley/index.html.

17. Mike McPhate, "California Today: Price Tag to Protect Speech at Berkeley: $600,000," *New York Times*, September 15, 2017, https://www.nytimes.com/2017/09/15/us/california-today-price -tag-to-protect-speech-at-berkeley-600000.html.

18. Daniel Henninger, "Liberals Are Eating Their Own," *Wall Street Journal*, April 3, 2019, https://www.wsj.com/articles /liberals-are-eating-their-own-11554332525.

19. Kaitlyn Schallhorn, "Feminists Protest Conservative Female Speaker, Retreat to 'Safe Space,'" *Campus Reform*, April 22, 2015, https://www.campusreform.org/?ID=6460.

20. Katie Reilly, "Conservative Writer Charles Murray Speaks Out against Middlebury Students Who Shut Down His Talk," *Time*, March 3, 2017, http://time.com/4690735/charles-murray -middlebury-protest/.

21. Heather Mac Donald, "The Hysterical Campus," Manhattan Institute, September 19, 2018, https://www.manhattan-institute .org/html/hysterical-campus-protests-university-free-speech .11482.html.

22. Heather Mac Donald, "The Hysterical Campus," *Quillette*, September 19, 2018 https://quillette.com/2018/09/19/the -hysterical-campus/.

23. Mac Donald, "Hysterical Campus."

24. Greg Lukianoff and Jonathan Haidt, "The Coddling of the American Mind," *Atlantic*, September 2015, https://www.the atlantic.com/magazine/archive/2015/09/the-coddling-of-the -american-mind/399356/.

25. Miriam Grossman, *Unprotected: A Campus Psychiatrist Reveals How Political Correctness in Her Profession Endangers Every Student* (New York: Penguin, 2006).

26. "Books by Dr. Jean Twenge," Dr. Jean Twenge, http://www .jeantwenge.com.

27. Jean Twenge and W. Keith Campbell, *The Narcissism Epiemic* (New York: Atria, 2013), 2.

28. Twenge and Campbell, *Narcissism Epidemic*, 68.

29. Peggy Drexler, "Millennials Are the Therapy Generation," *Wall Street Journal*, March 2–3, 2019, https://www.wsj.com/articles /millennials-are-the-therapy-generation-11551452286.

30. Joseph Bottum, "The Joy of Destruction," *Weekly Standard*, September 15, 2017, https://www.weeklystandard.com/joseph -bottum/the-joy-of-destruction-2009685.

31. Andrew O'Hehir, "America's First White President," *Salon*, December 10, 2016, https://www.salon.com/2016/12/10 /americas-first-white-president/.

32. Ta-Nehisi Coates, "The First White President," *Atlantic*, October 2017, https://www.theatlantic.com/magazine/archive/2017 /10/the-first-white-president-ta-nehisi-coates/537909/.

33. Not surprisingly, some targets repudiated the equation according to which nonprogressives—and even some progressives—collude whether knowingly or unknowingly with racism. Responding in the *Atlantic*, George Packer objected to treating "all white American political behavior as undifferentiated and founded on the idea of race." (George Packer, "George Packer Responds to Ta-Nehisi Coates," *Atlantic*, September 15, 2017, https://www .theatlantic.com/notes/2017/09/ta-nehisi-coates-george-packer -white-president/539976/.) Andrew Sullivan of *New York* criticized Coates for offering "one explanation only [for the election result of 2016]: white supremacism" and for "ignor[ing] other factors, such as Hillary Clinton's terrible candidacy, the populist revolt against immigration that had become a potent force across the West, and the possibility that the pace of social change might have triggered a

backlash among traditionalists." (Andrew Sullivan, "America Wasn't Built for Humans," *New York*, September 2017, http://nymag .com/intelligencer/2017/09/can-democracy-survive-tribalism .html.) Writing in the *Week*, Damon Linker added that "denouncing [Trump voters] all as racists is as unhelpful as it is inaccurate." (Damon Linker, "The Rise of Trump Isn't All about Racism," *Week*, September 12, 2017, https://theweek.com/articles/723854 /rise-trump-isnt-all-about-racism.)

34. Tom Lawson, "Female, Male or X? Canada Becomes the Tenth Country to Introduce Gender Neutral Passports," *Positive News*, September 8, 2017, https://www.positive.news/society/female -male-x-canada-becomes-tenth-country-introduce-gender -neutral-passports/.

35. Linley Sanders, "What Is Gender X? New Identity Is Accepted in These States, and Washington and Vermont Could Be Next," *Newsweek*, January 9, 2018, https://www.newsweek.com /gender-x-new-identity-states-washington-vermont-775221.

36. Astead W. Herndon, "Elizabeth Warren Apologizes to Cherokee Nation for DNA Test," *New York Times*, February 1, 2019, https://www .nytimes.com/2019/02/01/us/politics/elizabeth-warren-cherokee-dna .html.

37. Steve Kornacki, *The Red and the Blue: The 1990s and the Birth of Political Tribalism* (New York: Harper Collins, 2018).

38. George Packer, "A New Report Offers Insights into Tribalism in the Age of Trump," *New Yorker*, October 12, 2018, https://www.newyorker.com/news/daily-comment/a-new-report -offers-insights-into-tribalism-in-the-age-of-trump.

39. Amy Chua, *Political Tribes: Group Instinct and the Fate of Nations* (New York: Penguin Random House, 2018).

40. Andrew Sullivan, "America Wasn't Built for Humans."

41. See especially Christopher Lasch, *Haven in a Heartless World* (New York: Classic Books, 1978).

42. Erik H. Erikson, *Identity: Youth and Crisis* (New York: Norton, 1994), 75.

Chapter 2

1. "The Negro Family: The Case for National Action," Office of Planning and Research, United States Department of Labor, March 1965, https://web.stanford.edu/~mrosenfe/Moynihan%27s%20The%20Negro%20Family.pdf

2. James Q. Wilson, "Two Nations," AEI, December 4, 1997, http://www.aei.org/publication/two-nations/.

3. Elizabeth Marquardt, *Between Two Worlds: The Inner Lives of Children of Divorce* (New York: Three Rivers Press, 2005).

4. Mary Eberstadt, "Eminem Is Right," *Policy Review*, December 2004/January 2005, https://www.hoover.org/research/eminem-right.

5. "Emotionless by Good Charlotte," Songfacts, https://www.songfacts.com/facts/good-charlotte/emotionless.

6. Elizabeth Marquardt, Norval D. Glenn, and Karen Clark, *My Daddy's Name Is Donor: A New Study of Young Adults Conceived through Sperm Donation* (New York: Institute for American Values, 2010).

7. Ashley Fetters, "Finding the Lost Generation of Sperm Donors," *Atlantic*, May 18, 2018, https://www.theatlantic.com/family/archive/2018/05/sperm-donation-anonymous/560588/.

8. Madison Feller, "5 Women on Deciding Not to Have Children Because of Climate Change," *Elle*, October 19, 2018, https://www.elle.com/life-love/sex-relationships/a23837085/women-not-having-children-climate-change/.

9. Kristin Bialik, "Middle Children Have Become Rarer, But a Growing Share of Americans Now Say Three or More Kids Are 'Ideal,'" Pew Research Center, August 9, 2018, http://www.pewresearch.org/fact-tank/2018/08/09/middle-children-have-become-rarer-but-a-growing-share-of-americans-now-say-three-or-more-kids-are-ideal/.

10. M. E. Lamb et al., *Sibling Relationships: Their Nature and Significance across the Lifespan* (New York: Lawrence Erlbaum Associates, 1982).

11. Marc Jambon et al., "The Development of Empathetic Concern in Siblings: A Reciprocal Influence Model," *Child Development*, February 20, 2018, https://onlinelibrary.wiley.com/doi/full/10.1111/cdev.13015.

12. Donna Bobbitt-Zeher et al., "Number of Siblings During Childhood and the Likelihood of Divorce in Adulthood," *Journal of Family Issues* 37, no. 15 (2014): 2075–94, https://www.ncbi.nlm.nih .gov/pmc/articles/PMC5098899/.

13. Lamb and Sutton-Smith, *Sibling Relationships*, 350.

14. Ann Lukits, "Opposite-Sex Siblings Build Confidence in Romance," *Wall Street Journal*, November 9, 2015, https:// www.wsj.com/articles/opposite-sex-siblings-build-confidence-in -romance-1447085802.

15. Norimitsu Onishi, "A Generation in Japan Faces a Lonely Death," *New York Times*, November 30, 2017, https://www.ny times.com/2017/11/30/world/asia/japan-lonely-deaths-the-end .html.

16. Anna Fifield, "Japan's Lonely Deaths: A Growing Industry Is Now Devoted to Cleaning Up after Japanese People Dying Alone," *Independent*, January 30, 2018, https://www.independent .co.uk/news/long_reads/lonely-deaths-japan-die-alone-clean -apartments-japanese-industry-next-homes-clear-a8182861.html.

17. Michael Cosgrove, "Loneliness Is Becoming a Common Phenomena in France," *Le Figaro*, February 7, 2010, http://plus .lefigaro.fr/note/loneliness-is-becoming-a-common-phenomena -in-france-20100702-236888.

18. Felix Neto, "Socio-Demographic Predictors of Loneliness across the Adult Life Span in Portugal," *Interpersona* 8, no. 2 (2014), https://interpersona.psychopen.eu/article/view/171/html.

19. Guido Kleinhubbert and Angje Windmann, "Alone by the Millions: Isolation Crisis Threatens German Seniors," Spiegel Online, January 10, 2013, http//www.spiegel.de/international /germany/germany-faces-epidemic-of-lonely-and-isolated-seniors -a-876635.html.

20. Richard C. Keller, *Fatal Isolation: The Devastating Paris Heat Wave of 2003* (Chicago: University of Chicago Press, 2015).

21. John Tagliabue, "France to Study Why So Many Elderly Died in Heat Wave," *Chicago Tribune*, August 22, 2003, https://www .chicagotribune.com/news/ct-xpm-2003-08-22-0308210360-story .html.

22. Ellie Polack, "New Cigna Study Reveals Loneliness at Epidemic Levels in America," Cigna, May 1, 2018, https://www .cigna.com/newsroom/news-releases/2018/new-cigna-study -reveals-loneliness-at-epidemic-levels-in-america.

23. John T. Cacioppo and William Patrick, *Loneliness: Human Nature and the Need for Social Connection* (New York: W. W. Norton, 2008), 93.

24. Cacioppo and Patrick, *Loneliness*, 99–108.

25. Mary Eberstadt, *How the West Really Lost God: A New Theory of Secularization* (West Conshohocken, PA: Templeton Press, 2013).

26. Conor Clarke, "Why We Should Get Rid of Summer Vacation," *Atlantic*, June 7, 2009, https://www.theatlantic.com /politics/archive/2009/06/why-we-should-get-rid-of-summer -vacation/18902/. See also Geoffrey Canada, "Should the School Day be Longer?," *New York Times*, January 4, 2013, https://www.nytimes .com/roomfordebate/2011/09/26/should-the-school-day-be-longer /help-for-parents-and-society.

27. Jennifer McClellan, "One Third of Middle- and High-Schoolers Were Bullied Last Year, Study Shows," *USA Today*, September 24, 2018, https://www.usatoday.com/story/life/allthe moms/2018/09/24/one-out-three-students-were-bullied-us-school -last-year/1374631002/.

28. Jaana Juvonen, "School Violence: Prevalence, Fears, and Prevention," Rand Corporation, 2001, https://www.rand.org/pubs /issue_papers/IP219/index2.html.

29. Meg Anderson and Kavitha Cardoza, "Mental Health in Schools: A Hidden Crisis Affecting Millions of Students," NPR, August 31, 2016, https://www.npr.org/sections/ed/2016/08 /31/464727159/mental-health-in-schools-a-hidden-crisis-affecting -millions-of-students.

30. See, for example, Desmond Upton Patton et al., "Social Media as a Vector for Youth Violence: A Review of the Literature," *Computers in Human Behavior* 35 (June 2014): 548–553.

Chapter 3

1. Kirk Curnutt, "Fitzgerald Might Disagree With His 'No Second Acts' Line," interview by Audie Cornish, NPR, May 9, 2013, https://www.npr.org/2013/05/08/182337919/fitzgerald-might-disagree-with-his-no-second-acts-line.

2. Robert D. Putnam, *Bowling Alone: The Collapse and Revival of American Community* (New York: Simon and Schuster, 2000).

3. Francis Fukuyama, *Identity: The Demand for Dignity and the Politics of Resentment* (New York: Farrar, Straus and Giroux, 2018).

4. As cited in "What Is Cultural Appropriation and Why Is It Offensive?," *Week*, January 30, 2019, https://www.theweek.co.uk/cultural-appropriation.

5. Erika Christakis, "My Halloween Email Led to a Campus Firestorm—and a Troubling Lesson about Self-Censorship," *Washington Post*, October 28, 2016, https://www.washingtonpost.com/opinions/my-halloween-email-led-to-a-campus-firestorm--and-a-troubling-lesson-about-self-censorship/2016/10/28/70e55732-9b97-11e6-a0ed-ab0774c1eaa5_story.html?utm_term=.7537735ecc9c.

6. Robby Soave, "Campus Costume Cops Ask Students to Report 'Inappropriate' Halloween Costumes," *Daily Beast*, October 30, 2016, https://www.thedailybeast.com/campus-costume-cops-ask-students-to-report-inappropriate-halloween-costumes.

7. Avery Matera, "Victoria's Secret Accused of Cultural Appropriation for VS Show 2016 Costumes," *Teen Vogue*, December 1, 2016, https://www.teenvogue.com/story/victorias-secret-fashion-show-cultural-appropriation-chinese-vs-show-2016.

8. Vida Roberts, "BABY BAUBLE Pacifiers as Accessories Are Latest Trend on Fashion Front," *Baltimore Sun*, November 23, 1992, https://www.baltimoresun.com/news/bs-xpm-1992-11-23-1992328203-story.html.

9. Daniel Kahneman, Jack L. Knetsch, and Richard H. Thaler, "Anomalies: The Endowment Effect, Loss Aversion, and Status Bias," *Journal of Economic Perspectives* 5, no. 1 (Winter 1991): 193–206, https://www.aeaweb.org/articles?id=10.1257/jep.5.1.193.

10. https://www.identityevropa.com/terminology. This URL can no longer be accessed.

11. Nicole Goodkind, "Who Joins the Alt-Right? A Look at Charlottesville Anniversary," *Newsweek*, August 11, 2018, https://www.newsweek.com/charlottesville-anniversary-who-joins-alt-right-1067065.

12. Angela Nagle, *Kill All Normies: Online Culture Wars from 4Chan and Tumblr to Trump and the Alt-Right* (Hants, England: Zero Books, 2017), 67.

13. Niraj Chokshi, "What Is an Incel? A Term Used by the Toronto Van Attack Suspect, Explained," *New York Times*, April 24, 2018, https://www.nytimes.com/2018/04/24/world/canada/incel-reddit-meaning-rebellion.html.

14. Patt Morrison, "What We Need to Learn about Boys from the Violent Rise of the 'Incel Rebellion,'" *Los Angeles Times*, May 16, 2018, https://www.latimes.com/opinion/op-ed/la-ol-patt-morrison-warren-farrell-incel-20180516-htmlstory.html.

15. Colleen Flaherty, "Hijacking a Fundamental Right," *Inside Higher Ed*, March 21, 2017, https://www.insidehighered.com/news/2017/03/21/shouting-down-controversial-speaker-mcmaster-raises-new-concerns-about-academic.

16. Alexis Grenell, "White Women, Come Get Your People," *New York Times*, October 6, 2018, https://www.nytimes.com/2018/10/06/opinion/lisa-murkowski-susan-collins-kavanaugh.html.

Chapter 4

1. Mary Eberstadt, "How Protests against Donald Trump Reveal a Class Divide," *Time*, February 15, 2017, http://time.com/4671085/eberstadt-trump-protests/.

2. Susan Sontag, "Notes on 'Camp,'" Georgetown University, 1964, https://faculty.georgetown.edu/irvinem/theory/Sontag-NotesOnCamp-1964.html.

3. "Miley Cyrus Presents," August 29, 2014, *V Magazine*, https://vmagazine.com/article/miley-cyrus-presents/.

4. The Root, "bell hooks: Beyonce Is a Terrorist," *Ebony*, May 9, 2014, https://www.ebony.com/news/bell-hooks-beyonce-is-a-terrorist-981/.

5. Anna Breslaw, "The Unfuckables," *New Inquiry*, May 10, 2012, https://thenewinquiry.com/author/anna-breslaw/.

6. Anna North, "Should 'Slut' Be Retired?," *New York Times*, February 3, 2015, https://op-talk.blogs.nytimes.com/2015/02/03/should-slut-be-retired/.

7. Julia Long, "Pornography Is More Than Just Sexual Fantasy. It's Cultural Violence," *Washington Post*, May 27, 2016, https://www.washingtonpost.com/news/in-theory/wp/2016/05/27/pornography-is-more-than-just-sexual-fantasy-its-cultural-violence/?utm_term=.f8bb467f30fd.

8. There is also the trash-talking and purported tell-all adventuring that has become a genre unto itself—Lena Dunham's *Not That Kind of Girl: A Young Woman Tells You What She's "Learned"* and Michelle Tea's *The Passionate Mistakes and Intricate Corruption of One Girl in America* and related works. Fans of these kinds of confessionals are legion enough to suggest that the appetite for watching women debase themselves—and one another—just might be insatiable too.

Chapter 5

1. Sandhya Somaschekhar, "A Question for Schools: Which Sports Teams Should Transgender Students Play On?," *Washington Post*, October 2, 2014, https://www.washingtonpost.com/politics/a-question-for-schools-which-sports-teams-should-transgender-students-play-on/2014/10/02/d3f33b06-49c7-11e4-b72e-d60a9229cc10_story.html?utm_term=.fd7cb32159bd.

2. "Makeup for Men: The Future of Cosmetics?," Hims, https://www.forhims.com/blog/makeup-for-men.

3. See, for example, the case studies in Ryan T. Anderson's *When Harry Became Sally: Responding to the Transgender Moment* (New York: Encounter Books, 2018).

4. See, for example, Rowan Scarborough, "Pressure Grows on Marines to Consider Lowering Combat Standards for Women,"

Washington Times, April 19, 2015, https://www.washingtontimes.com
/news/2015/apr/19/marine-corps-weighs-lower-standards-for
-women-afte/, and Dave Collins and Lisa Maria Pane, "Police Loosen
Standards for Accepting Recruits," PoliceOne.com, November 15,
2016,   https://www.policeone.com/police-jobs-and-careers/articles
/241023006-Police-loosen-standards-for-accepting-recruits/.

5. Tyler Pager, "Drafting Only Men for the Military Is
Unconstitutional, Judge Rules," *New York Times*, February 24, 2019,
https://www.nytimes.com/2019/02/24/us/military-draft-men
-unconstitutional.html.

6. Ashley McGuire, *Sex Scandal: The Drive to Abolish Male and
Female* (Washington, DC: Regnery, 2017).

7. "Gender-Bending Fashion Spotted at Tokyo Fashion Week
Bang on Trend," *Fashion United*, March 27, 2017, https://fashion
united.uk/news/fashion/gender-bending-fashion-spotted-at-tokyo
-fashion-week-bang-on-trend/2017032723995.

8. Tokyo Fashion, "Genderless Kei—Japan's Hot New
Fashion Trend," *Medium*, January 29, 2016, https://medium.com
/@TokyoFashion/genderless-kei-japan-s-hot-new-fashion-trend
-9e25a2c559c6.

9. Tokyo Fashion, "Genderless Kei."

10. Riaan Jacob George, "Tracing the Rise of Androgyny in
Indian Menswear," *Verve*, July 22, 2016, http://www.vervemagazine
.in/fashion-and-beauty/androgyny-indian-fashion-menswear.

11. Cheryl-Ann Couto, "Genderless Fashion: Indian Designers
Are Changing the Way We Look at Clothes," *Scroll.in*, February 27,
2018,   https://scroll.in/magazine/869124/genderless-fashion-indian
-designers-are-changing-the-way-we-look-at-clothes.

12. "In China and India, Men Outnumber women on a massive Scale," *Washington Post*, April 24, 2018, https://www.washington
post.com/graphics/2018/world/too-many-men/?utm_term=
.ba1c2ad5f091.

13. Alexandra Harney, "The Herbivore's Dilemma," *Slate*, June
15, 2009, https://slate.com/news-and-politics/2009/06/japan-panics
-about-the-rise-of-herbivores-young-men-who-shun-sex-don-t
-spend-money-and-like-taking-walks.html.

14. Marian Liu and Serenitie Wang, "China's All-Girl Boy Band," CNN, May 12, 2017, https://www.cnn.com/2017/04/27 /entertainment/china-acrush-boy-band-androgny/index.html.

15. Abid Rahman, "Meet the Oprah of China, Who Happens to Be Transgender," *Hollywood Reporter*, November 1, 2016, https://www.hollywoodreporter.com/features/meet-oprah-china -who-happens-be-transgender-942750.

16. Hans Villarica, "Study of the Day: Why Men Want Sons and Women Want Daughters," *Atlantic*, January 18, 2012, https:// www.theatlantic.com/health/archive/2012/01/study-of-the-day -why-men-want-sons-and-women-want-daughters/250972/.

17. Britni de al Cretaz, "More Girls Are Playing Football: Is That Progress?," *New York Times*, February 2, 2018, https://www.ny times.com/2018/02/02/well/family/football-girls-concussions.html.

18. Robert H. Shmerling, "The Gender Gap in Sports Injuries," *Harvard Health Blog*, December 3, 2015, https://www.health .harvard.edu/blog/the-gender-gap-in-sports-injuries-2015 12038708.

19. Alex Flanagan, "The Effect Terrible Sports Dads Have on Everyone's Daughters," May 13, 2017, https://ilovetowatchyouplay .com/2017/05/13/effect-terrible-sports-dads-everyones-daughters/.

20. Lionel Tiger, *The Decline of Males: The First Look at an Unexpected New World for Men and Women* (New York: St. Martin's Press, 1999).

21. Emiko Jozuka, "Why Won't 541,000 Young Japanese Men Leave the House?," CNN, September 12, 2016, https://www.cnn .com/2016/09/11/asia/japanese-millennials-hikikomori-social -recluse/index.html.

22. Kim Min-Kwan and Esther Chung, "More Koreans Become Recluses," *Korea JoongAng Daily*, January 23, 2017, http://korea joongangdaily.joins.com/news/article/article.aspx?aid=3028993.

23. Maya Salem, "What Is Toxic Masculinity?," *New York Times*, January 22, 2019, https://www.nytimes.com/2019/01/22/us /toxic-masculinity.html.

24. Kelefa Sanneh, "Jordan Peterson's Gospel of Masculinity,"

New Yorker, February 26, 2018, https://www.newyorker.com /magazine/2018/03/05/jordan-petersons-gospel-of-masculinity.

25. Andrew Reiner, "The Fear of Having a Son," *New York Times*, October 14, 2016, https://www.nytimes.com/2016/10/14 /well/family/the-fear-of-having-a-son.html.

Chapter 6

1. For introductions to Girard's thought, see, for example, Joe Carter, "How to Read Girard," *First Things*, July 16, 2009, https://www.firstthings.com/blogs/firstthoughts/2009/07/how -to-read-girard; René Girard, "An Interview with René Girard," interview by Grant Kaplan, *First Things*, November 6, 2008, https:// www.firstthings.com/web-exclusives/2008/11/an-interview-with -rene-girard; Edward T. Oakes, "René Girard for Holy Week," *First Things*, April 5, 2007, https://www.firstthings.com/web-exclusives /2007/04/rene-girard-for-holy-week. See also the website of Imitatio (http://www.imitatio.org), an institute founded by former student Peter Thiel and others "to press forward the consequences of Rene Girard's remarkable insights into human behavior and culture."

2. Bennett G. Galef and Kevin N. Laland, "Social Learning in Animals: Empirical Studies and Theoretical Models," *Bio-Science* 55, no. 6 (2005), https://academic.oup.com/bioscience /article/55/6/489/363397.

3. "6 Important Life Skills That Mother Cats Teach Their Kittens," Pets4Homes, https://www.pets4homes.co.uk/pet-advice /6-important-life-skills-that-mother-cats-teach-their-kittens .html.

4. Temple Grandin and Catherine Johnson, *Animals Make Us Human*, Ibid, 97.

5. Alex Thornton and Nichola J. Raihani, "The Evolution of Teaching," *Animal Behaviour* 75 (2008): 1823–36, http://www .mbe-erice.org/papers/2015-thornton-and-raihani.pdf.

6. Ibid.

7. John T. Cacioppo & William Patrick, *Loneliness: Human Nature and the Need for Social Connection* (New York: W.W. Norton,

2008), 129–130.

8. Cacioppo & Patrick, *Loneliness.*

9. Cacioppo & Patrick, *Loneliness.*

10. Arthur C. Brooks, *Who Really Cares: The Surprising Truth about Compassionate Conservatism* (New York: Basic Books, 2006).

11. For a summary, see Mary Eberstadt, *How the West Really Lost God: A New Theory of Secularization* (West Conshohocken, PA: Templeton Press, 2013), 197–99 and footnotes 10–19.

12. Harold G. Koenig, Michael E. McCullough, and David B. Larsen, *Handbook of Religion and Health* (New York: Oxford University Press, 2001).

13. Robert A. Hummer, Richard G. Rogers, Charles B. Nam, and Christopher G. Ellison, "Religious Involvement and U.S. Adult Mortality," *Demography* 36, no. 2 (May 1999): 283.

14. David Shultz, "Divorce Rates Double When People Start Watching Porn," *Science*, August 26, 2016, https://www.sciencemag.org/news/2016/08/divorce-rates-double-when-people-start-watching-porn.

15. Mark Regnerus, *Cheap Sex: The Transformation of Men, Marriage, and Monogamy* (New York: Oxford Universisty Press, 2017).

16. Regnerus, *Cheap Sex.*

17. J. Freedom du Lac, Amy B. Wang, and Marwa Eltagouri, "'I Am Not Okay': The Remarkable Response to the Charlie Rose Allegations, from His CBS Colleagues," *Washington Post*, November 21, 2017, https://www.washingtonpost.com/news/arts-and-entertainment/wp/2017/11/21/i-am-not-okay-cbs-this-mornings-remarkable-response-to-the-charlie-rose-allegations/?utm_term=.b2c252ad0e3f.

18. CBSNews.com Staff, "The Delinquents: A Spate of Rhino Killings," *60 Minutes*, August 22, 2000, https://www.cbsnews.com/news/the-delinquents/.

Conclusion

1. Endorsement for G. A. Bradshaw's *Elephants on the Edge: What*

Animals Teach Us about Humility (New Haven, CT: Yale University Press, 2009).

2. G. A. Bradshaw et al., "Elephant Breakdown," *Nature* 433, no. 807 (2005), https://www.nature.com/articles/433807a.

3. Charles Siebert, "An Elephant Crackup?," *New York Times Magazine*, October 8, 2006, https://www.nytimes.com/2006/10/08/magazine/08elephant.html

4. Siebert, "An Elephant Crackup?"

5. Siebert, "An Elephant Crackup?"

6. Jennifer Senior, "Teen Fiction and the Perils of Cancel Culture," *New York Times*, March 8, 2019, https://www.nytimes.com/2019/03/08/opinion/teen-fiction-and-the-perils-of-cancel-culture.html.

7. "LGBT Group Severs Links with Navratilova over Transgender Comments," BBC, February 20, 2019, https://www.bbc.com/news/world-us-canada-47301007.

8. Laura Lambert, "Novelist Ian McEwan Climbs Down amid Transgender Outcry: Author Faces Further Criticism from Some Groups about His Decision to Backtrack," *Daily Mail*, April 7, 2016, https://www.dailymail.co.uk/news/article-3529255/Novelist-Ian-McEwan-climbs-amid-transgender-outcry-Author-faces-criticism-groups-decision-backtrack.html.

9. These include books like Pascal Bruckner's *The Tyranny of Guilt*, Pierre Manent's *Beyond Radical Secularism*, Douglas Murray's *The Strange Death of Europe*, and the novels of Michel Houellebecq, who has become the chief literary cartographer in fictional form of the sexual revolution's effects.

10. Mary Eberstadt, *Adam and Eve after the Pill: Paradoxes of the Sexual Revolution* (San Francisco: Ignatius Press, 2012).

11. Claire Cain Miller, "How Did Marriage Become a Mark of Privilege?," *New York Times*, September 25, 2017, https://www.nytimes.com/2017/09/25/upshot/how-did-marriage-become-a-mark-of-privilege.html.

12. Rod Dreher, *The Benedict Option: A Strategy for Christians in a Post-Christian Nation* (New York: Penguin Random House, 2017).

13. Mary Eberstadt, "Viewpoint: In the War over Christianity, Orthodoxy Is Winning," *Time*, April 29, 2013, http://ideas.time.com/2013/04/29/viewpoint-in-the-war-over-christianity-orthodoxy-is-winning/.

14. See, for example, Laurence Iannacccone, "Why Strict Churches Are Strong," *American Journal of Sociology* 99, no. 5 (March 1994): 1180–1211. See also Eric Kaufmann, *Shall the Religious Inherit the Earth? Demography and Politics in the Twenty-First Century* (London: Profile Books, 2011).

Rod Dreher

1. Bryan Ward-Perkins, *The Fall of Rome: And the End of Civilization* (Oxford: Oxford University Press, 2005).

2. Jane Jacobs, *Dark Age Ahead* (New York: Random House, 2004).

3. Jacobs, *Dark Age*.

4. Carle Zimmerman, *Family and Civilization* (Wilmington, DE: Intercollegiate Studies Institute, 2008).

5. Zimmerman, *Family and Civilization*.

6. Mary Eberstadt, *How the West Really Lost God: A New Theory of Secularization* (West Conshohocken, PA: Templeton Press, 2013).

7. The term "Moralistic Therapeutic Deism" (MTD) is taken from Christian Smith, with Melinda Lundquist Denton, *Soul Searching: The Religious and Spiritual Lives of American Teenagers*, 9 (Oxford and New York: Oxford University Press, 2005).

8. Christian Smith, "On 'Moralistic Therapeutic Deism' as U.S. Teenagers' Actual, Tacit, De Facto Religious Faith," In *Princeton Lectures on Youth, Church, and Culture*, Princeton, NJ: Princeton Theological Seminary (2005).

9. For more detail about the Benedict Option, see Rod Dreher, *The Benedict Option: A Strategy for Christians in a Post-Christian Nation* (New York: Penguin Random House, 2017).

Mark Lilla

1. Mark Lilla, *The Once and Future Liberal: After Identity Politics* (New York: HarperCollins, 2017).

2. Anna Fifield, "Beijing's One-Child Policy Is Gone. But Many Chinese Are Still Reluctant to Have More," May 4, 2019, *Washington Post*, https://www.washingtonpost.com/world/asia_pacific/beijings-one-child-policy-is-gone-but-many-chinese-are-still-reluctant-to-have-more/2019/05/02/c722e568-604f-11e9-bf24-db4b9fb62aa2_story.html?utm_term=.46172d26c496.

3. Zygmunt Bauman, *Liquid Love* (Cambridge, England: Polity Press, 2003).

Bibliography

Books discussed in *Primal Screams*:

Anderson, Ryan T. *When Harry Became Sally: Responding to the Transgender Movement*. New York: Encounter Books, 2018.

Bawer, Bruce. *The Victims' Revolution: The Rise of Identity Studies and the Closing of the Liberal Mind*. New York: Broadside Books, 2012.

Bloom, Allan. *The Closing of the American Mind*. New York: Simon and Schuster, 1987.

Bradshaw, G. A. *Elephants on the Edge: What Animals Teach Us about Humility*. New Haven, CT: Yale University Press, 2009.

Brooks, Arthur C. *Who Really Cares: The Surprising Truth about Compassionate Conservatism*. New York: Basic Books, 2006.

Cacioppo, John T., and William Patrick. *Loneliness: Human Nature and the Need for Social Connection*. New York: W. W. Norton, 2008.

Chua, Amy. *Political Tribes: Group Instinct and the Fate of Nations*. New York: Penguin Random House, 2018.

Dreher, Rod. *The Benedict Option: A Strategy for Christians in a Post-Christian Nation.* New York: Penguin Random House, 2017.

Eberstadt, Mary. *Adam and Eve after the Pill: Paradoxes of the Sexual Revolution.* San Francisco: Ignatius Press, 2012.

———. *Home-Alone America.* New York: Sentinel, 2004.

———. *How the West Really Lost God: A New Theory of Secularization.* West Conshohocken, PA: Templeton Press, 2013.

———. *It's Dangerous to Believe: Religious Freedom and Its Enemies* New York: Harper, 2016.

Erikson, Erik H. *Identity: Youth and Crisis.* New York: Norton, 1994.

Fukuyama, Francis. *Identity: The Demand for Dignity and the Politics of Resentment.* New York: Farrar, Straus and Giroux, 2018.

Gitlin, Todd. *The Twilight of Common Dreams: Why America Is Wracked by Culture Wars.* New York: Holt, 1996.

Grandin, Temple, and Catherine Johnson. *Animals Make Us Human: Creating the Best Life for Animals.* Boston: Mariner Books, 2009.

Grossman, Miriam. *Unprotected: A Campus Psychiatrist Reveals How Political Correctness in Her Profession Endangers Every Student.* New York: Penguin, 2006.

Keller, Richard C. *Fatal Isolation: The Devastating Paris Heat Wave of 2003.* Chicago: University of Chicago Press, 2015.

Koenig, Harold G., Michael E. McCullough, and David B. Larsen. *Handbook of Religion and Health.* New York: Oxford University Press, 2001.

Kornacki, Steve. *The Red and the Blue: The 1990s and the Birth of Political Tribalism.* New York: HarperCollins, 2018.

Lamb, Michael E., and Brian Sutton Smith. *Sibling Relationships: Their Nature and Significance across the Lifespan.* New York: Lawrence Erlbaum Associates, 1982.

Lasch, Christopher. *Haven in a Heartless World.* New York: Norton, 1995.

Lilla, Mark. *The Once and Future Liberal: After Identity Politics.* New York: HarperCollins, 2017.

Marquardt, Elizabeth. *Between Two Worlds: The Inner Lives of Children of Divorce*. New York: Three Rivers Press, 2005.

Marquardt, Elizabeth, Norval D. Glenn, and Karen Clark, *My Daddy's Name Is Donor* (New York: Institute for American Values, 2010).

McGuire, Ashley. *Sex Scandal: The Drive to Abolish Male and Female*. Washington, DC: Regnery, 2017.

Murray, Douglas. *The Strange Death of Europe: Immigration, Identity, Islam* London: Bloomsbury Continuum, 2017.

Nagle, Angela. *Kill All Normies: Online Culture Wars from 4Chan and Tumblr to Trump and the Alt-Right*. Hants, England: Zero Books, 2017.

Nietzsche, Friedrich. *The Gay Science, Book III*.

Putnam, Robert D. *Bowling Alone: The Collapse and Revival of American Community*. New York: Simon and Schuster, 2000.

Regnerus, Mark. *Cheap Sex: The Transformation of Men, Marriage, and Monogamy*. New York: Oxford, 2017.

Schlesinger, Arthur Meier. *The Disuniting of America: Reflections on a Multicultural Society*. London: W. W. Norton, 1998.

Tiger, Lionel. *The Decline of Males: The First Look at an Unexpected New World for Men and Women*. New York: St. Martin's Press, 1999.

Twinge, Jean, and W. Keith Campbell. *The Narcissism Epidemic*. New York: Atria, 2013.

About the Contributors

Rod Dreher is a senior editor at the *American Conservative*. He has been a columnist or editor for the *New York Post*, the *Dallas Morning News*, *National Review*, and others. He is the author of four books, including the *New York Times* bestsellers *The Little Way of Ruthie Leming* (2013) and *The Benedict Option* (2017). He lives in Baton Rouge, Louisiana, with his wife Julie and their three children.

Mary Eberstadt is an American writer and a Senior Research Fellow at the Faith and Reason Institute in Washington, D.C. Her books include *How the West Really Lost God: A New Theory of Secularization*; *It's Dangerous to Believe: Religious Freedom and Its Enemies*; *Adam and Eve after the Pill: Paradoxes of the Sexual Revolution*; and the novel *The Loser Letters: A Comic Tale of Life, Death, and Atheism*.

Mark Lilla is professor of the Humanities at Columbia University and a longstanding contributor to the *New York Review* *of Books*. His most recent books are *The Shipwrecked Mind: On Political Reaction* (2016) and *The Once and Future Liberal: After Identity Politics* (2017).

PETER THIEL is an entrepreneur and investor. He cofounded PayPal, led it as CEO, and took it public; he made the first outside investment in Facebook, where he serves as a director; and he cofounded Palantir Technologies, where he serves as chairman. He has provided early funding for LinkedIn, Yelp, and dozens of startups, many run by former colleagues who have been dubbed the "PayPal Mafia." He is a partner at Founders Fund, a Silicon Valley venture capital firm that has funded companies including SpaceX and Airbnb. He started the Thiel Fellowship, which funds young entrepreneurs, and he leads the Thiel Foundation, which works to advance technological progress and long-term thinking. He is also the #1 *New York Times* bestselling author of *Zero to One: Notes on Startups, or How to Build the Future*.

Index